Selection of translated essays from the German exhibition catalog

THE COLLECTOR CURT GLASER

FROM CHAMPION OF MODERNISM TO REFUGEE

Edited by
Anita Haldemann and Judith Rauser

Deutscher Kunstverlag

kunstmuseum basel

FOREWORD

In May 1933, the Kunstmuseum Basel acquired two hundred drawings and prints from the collection of Curt Glaser (1879–1943) for the Kupferstichkabinett at an auction in Berlin. After the Nazis seized power, Glaser was ousted as the director of the Kunstbibliothek (Art Library) in Berlin because of his Jewish origins, thus ending his professional career in Germany. In May 1933, he therefore decided to sell at auction most of the extensive art collection he had built up with his wife Elsa Glaser, née Kolker (1878–1932), who had died the previous year. He then emigrated to Switzerland in the summer of 1933 with his second wife Maria Glaser, née Milch (1901–1981). The couple moved on to New York in 1941, where Glaser died in 1943.

In 2004, the Glaser heirs contacted the Kunstmuseum Basel for the first time and soon laid claim to all of the two hundred works. In March 2020, they reached an agreement with the Canton of Basel-Stadt for a "just and fair solution" in accordance with the Washington Principles (Washington Conference Principles on Nazi-Confiscated Art). As part of this solution, the museum retained the artworks but compensated the heirs financially; in addition, both agreed to commemorate Glaser's fate in an extensive exhibition, which is generously supported by the government of the Canton of Basel-Stadt.

An account of the historical facts of the "Glaser case" and its assessment in accordance with the Washington Principles has been made permanently available on the homepage of the Kunstmuseum. Nonetheless, we feel it is crucial to supplement the exhibition with a comprehensive publication in order to make a lasting statement against forgetting. As a private collector, art historian, critic, curator at the Berlin Kupferstichkabinett (Department of Prints and Drawings), and later director of the Berlin Kunstbibliothek, Curt Glaser was one of the most distinguished and influential players in the art world of the Weimar Republic; yet in the postwar period, his achievements and his fate faded into obscurity. This exhibition and catalog pay tribute to Glaser's contribution to art history and commemorate his persecution by the Nazis and his exile in Switzerland, and later in New York. To the extent it can be reconstructed, the role played in his life and career by his two wives is also taken into account. At the same time, the exhibition is also dedicated to the history of Curt and Elsa Glaser's extensive and significant collection, which is now dispersed among numerous museums and private owners. With two hundred works on paper, the Kupferstichkabinett of the Kunstmuseum Basel holds the largest coherent body of works from Glaser's former collection, which forever links the Öffentliche Kunstsammlung Basel to Glaser's fate in an exceptional way and puts the museum in his debt.

When the works were acquired in 1933, the Kunstmuseum building on St. Alban-Graben did not yet exist, but its construction was being planned. Otto Fischer, who became head of the Öffentliche Kunstsammlung Basel in 1928, was to lead the institution out of the cramped spaces in Augustinergasse on the Münsterhügel and into the modern age while respecting its long tradition. Thus, the acquisition of modern, especially contemporary art was a great aspiration that gave rise to intense discussions.

This background for the purchase of works from Glaser's collection at a time when prices were relatively low is a part of the story of the Öffentliche Kunstsammlung Basel that needs to be told. The reappraisal of the historical facts was carried out when the Kunstmuseum Basel did not yet have a department for provenance research but could only count on support from the Federal Office of Culture for the reappraisal of collection acquisitions from the years 1933 to 1945. The decision to assess the facts in-house was motivated by the desire to work through and understand the history of our institution and the development of the collection in all of its both wonderful yet problematic aspects, and to permanently embed these insights in the institution.

It should also be noted that concurrently with the exhibition on Curt Glaser, another show relevant to this context is also on view at the Kunstmuseum Basel: *Castaway Modernism: Basel's Acquisitions of "Degenerate" Art*, organized by Eva

Reifert (Curator of Nineteenth-Century and Modern Art) and Tessa Rosebrock (Head of Provenance Research). It is devoted to Georg Schmidt, the successor to Otto Fischer, and his purchases in 1939 of modern art that had been defamed as "degenerate" and forcibly removed from German museums. It, too, presents an important chapter of Basel's collection history to the public for the first time in all of its facets.

The Kunstmuseum Basel and the Kunstkommission [Art Commission] chaired by Felix Uhlmann consider the decision and the agreement reached in the Glaser case as representative of a fundamental commitment of the museum to provenance research and to the Washington Principles. The publication of the report, which includes the legal and historical basis of the decision, was received positively in the Swiss and international context as an example of best practices. It was not least because of this experience with the "Glaser case" that a department for provenance research staffed with the appropriate expertise could be gradually built up over the past three years with a great deal of in-house commitment and financial support from the Ernst Göhner Foundation and the Canton of Basel-Stadt.

First and foremost, we would like to thank the community of Curt Glaser's heirs, especially Valerie Sattler and Bettina Meyer Basanow, for their generous support of our research through their illuminating reports on the context family history and the provision of invaluable photographic material from the family archive, which was not accessible when the 2018 report was written. In addition, Edvard Munch's double portrait of Elsa and Curt Glaser can now be exhibited in Basel for the first time. Curt and Maria Glaser had left it on deposit at the Kunstmuseum Basel, and it continues to be the property of the community of heirs to this day.

We would like to thank especially Laurie A. Stein and the numerous other provenance researchers and curatorial colleagues in Europe and the United States who advised us on this project and contributed concrete historical information to help expand our knowledge of Glaser's biography and fate, and provide the factual basis required for the development of the ultimate decision. In addition, our research was actively supported by Noemi Scherrer (former research assistant at the Kupferstichkabinett), Rainer Baum (Head of Library and Archive), Joanna Smalcerz (former research assistant at the Provenance Research Department), Tessa Rosebrock, Ralph Ubl (University of Basel), Felix Uhlmann (President of the Board of Trustees of the Kunstmuseum Basel), Gunhild Pörksen (Archive, Ita Wegman Institut für anthroposophische Grundlagenforschung, Arlesheim), Niklaus Hottinger (Archive Sonnenhof, Arlesheim) and Rebecca Birrer (research assistant, Kunsthalle Basel, Archive and Photo Archive).

We are particularly indebted to the partner institutions that have supported this exhibition catalog with research and written contributions and have entrusted us with valuable loans for the exhibition. First and foremost, we would like to mention our collaborators at the institutions where Glaser worked in Berlin: Dagmar Korbacher and Andreas Schalhorn, Kupferstichkabinett, Staatliche Museen zu Berlin—Preußischer Kulturbesitz; and Moritz Wullen and Joachim Brand, Kunstbibliothek, Staatliche Museen zu Berlin—Preußischer Kulturbesitz. We would also like to thank the following lenders and authors: James Rondeau, The Art Institute of Chicago; Alexander Klar and Andreas Stolzenburg, Hamburger Kunsthalle; Yilmaz Dziewor, Museum Ludwig, Cologne; Deborah Swallow, Alexandra Gerstein, and Ketty Gottardo, The Courtauld, London; Lynn Rother and Max Koss, Leuphana University Lüneburg; Katherine Crawford Luber, Minneapolis Institute of Art; Mary Ceruti, Walker Art Center, Minneapolis; Colin Bailey, John Marciari, and Jennifer Tonkovich, The Morgan Library & Museum, New York; Deborah Diemente, Smith College Museum of Art, Northampton; Min Jung Kim, Saint Louis Art Museum; Christoph Becker, Philippe Büttner, and Joachim Sieber, Kunsthaus Zürich.

Our thanks also go to Kathleen Herfurth and Luzie Diekmann from the publishing house Deutscher Kunstverlag for their exceptional efforts; Michael Konze and Rebecca van Dyck for their careful editing; and Verena Gerlach for the outstanding graphic design of the publication.

In-house, we would like to thank all our colleagues who worked intensively on this exhibition project and the publication, especially Judith Rauser, assistant curator at the Kupferstichkabinett, who organized the exhibition as co-curator with Anita Haldemann; and our curatorial intern Amanda Kopp.

Josef Helfenstein

Director, Kunstmuseum Basel

Anita Haldemann

Head of Art & Research and Deputy Director
Head, Kupferstichkabinett
(Department of Prints and Drawings)

Anita Haldemann
Noemi Scherrer

CURT GLASER—FROM THE CENTER OF BERLIN'S ART WORLD TO EMIGRATION

On November 25, 1943, an obituary appeared in the *New York Times* with the headline: "Dr. Curt Glaser, Art Authority, 64; German Refugee, Ex-Director of State Art Library of Berlin Museums, Dies Up-State".[1] The German-Jewish art historian Curt Glaser (1879–1943) had lost his position as Director of the Berlin Kunstbibliothek (Art Library) ten years earlier, after the Nazis rose to power (p. 10). He then dissolved his household and, in May 1933, had to auction off the immense art collection and library that he had built up together with his first wife Elsa Kolker (1878–1932) in order to leave Germany forever. Thus ended the career of one of the most important and distinguished art historians of the Weimar Republic. Although the widower and his second wife, Maria Milch (1901–1981), enjoyed a happy private life in emigration, he was not able to gain a foothold professionally despite his attempts to do so after the relocation to New York. However, his reputation as an authority on art, which had reached all the way to the United States thanks to his international network and his far-reaching publication record, remained intact.

In the decades following his death, despite his great importance as an art historian, critic, museum leader, and collector, he largely fell into obscurity. At fault for the patchiness of his later reception is not just the radical break in his career that he experienced in emigration but also the loss of many archives during the war. Interest in him first reawakened in the 1990s in his old sphere of influence in Berlin, when the sinologist and library director at the Staatsbibliothek Berlin, Hartmut Walravens, drew attention to Glaser's scholarly work on the art history of East Asia.[2] Andreas Strobl's 2006 biography of Glaser, which primarily paid tribute to his comprehensive achievements as an art historian and critic, was the first to provide a comprehensive picture of him.[3] This was followed by the significant essay in 2012 by Joachim Brand and Hein-Th. Schulze Altcappenberg in the *Jahrbuch Preußischer Kulturbesitz*.[4]

In the meantime, our state of knowledge about Curt Glaser has advanced in many institutions and among provenance researchers, primarily in conjunction with the process of finding just and fair solutions for compensation claims brought by his community of heirs. Although large gaps still remain, thanks to intensive research and rediscovered documents, we now have a much more comprehensive picture of Glaser's life and work, which this essay will honor. The Kunstmuseum Basel has made available on the homepage of its website its appraisal of the historical facts relating to the acquisition of two hundred artworks from the former estate of Curt Glaser. This document has been updated in certain points with a view to the present publication.[5]

FIRST BIOGRAPHICAL STATIONS

Curt Glaser was born to a Jewish family in Leipzig on May 29, 1879. His parents, the merchant Simon Glaser (1841–1904) and Emma Glaser, née Haase (1854–1927),[6] had two other children. Glaser's brother Felix (1874–1931), older by five years, was a physician and died unexpectedly early at the age of fifty-seven. His younger brother Paul (1885–1946), an art and antiquities dealer, lost his life in exile in Brazil.[7]

After his family moved to Berlin in 1886, Curt Glaser attended the Königliches Wilhelms-Gymnasium in the fashionable Tiergarten district, graduating in 1897. He subsequently completed his medical studies in Munich at the Ludwig-Maximilians-Universität and received his doctorate degree in 1902. However, he would never practice medicine except briefly during his military service. Instead he began his study of art history immediately after receiving his medical degree. This was a bold decision, because the career he aimed for in the Prussian civil service was a precarious endeavor, as Jews were massively disadvantaged compared to Christians. The medical path would have been far less risky and would have guaranteed social standing.[8]

It is likely that his impending marriage to his cousin and exact contemporary Elsa Kolker had a decidedly positive influence on his decision to take this step (p. 25).[9] Coming from an upper-middle-class background, Elsa was self-confident, educated, and intellectually curious. She brought a considerable fortune to the match, which was formalized on August 12, 1903. Contemporaries reported that Elsa was overwhelmingly responsible for the couple's social standing.[10] In addition, she contributed conceptually as well as financially to the building of their art collection. It can otherwise hardly be explained how the pair had already come to purchase a painting by Vincent van Gogh in 1904, which they then sold again in 1914, and could afford another ambitious purchase of a Henri Matisse painting in 1912 (p. 83).[11]

GLASER'S CAREER AS AN ART HISTORIAN AND PRIVATE COLLECTOR

Glaser took up the study of art history in Berlin in 1902. His career as an author began at the same time. Since he had already been engaged with art for some time, that same year he began working as a critic.[12] Until October 1910, he wrote reviews of art exhibitions in Berlin for the *Hamburgischer Correspondent*, and starting in 1909, for the journal *Kunst und Künstler* edited by Karl Scheffler (1869–1951), as well as for *Kunstchronik*, the supplement to the *Zeitschrift für bildende Kunst* (published by Seemann Verlag, Leipzig). In 1919 he became the *Kunstchronik's* Berlin editor and finally, in 1922, its publisher.[13] In 1918, together with Scheffler, he conceived the book series *Deutsche Meister*, published by Insel-Verlag.[14] That same November, he began writing for the *Berliner Börsen-Courier*.

Glaser's studies included sojourns in Munich and Freiburg, where he studied with Karl Voll (art history) and Adolf Furtwängler (archaeology). He earned his doctorate in 1907 in Berlin under Heinrich Wölfflin (1864–1945), professor at the Friedrich-Wilhelms-Universität, and published his dissertation on Hans Holbein the Elder in 1908.[15] The following year, Glaser began his professional museum career as a "research assistant" at the Königliches Kupferstichkabinett Berlin, where he remained until the end of September 1918.[16]

During his employment at the Kupferstichkabinett, Curt and Elsa Glaser took trips to Paris in 1910 and 1912, and then to Oslo in 1913 to visit Edvard Munch (1863–1944) for the first time (pp. 22, 26 top). In 1911, they spent April through November traveling in Japan, and probably also in China. As he reported in an article on Claude Monet in 1930, Glaser had already visited the Japanese section of the Paris World's Fair in 1900.[17] Thanks to this intensive engagement and his profound sensibilities, Glaser was able to break away from the Eurocentric perspective and do justice to the particularities of East Asian art history in his publications on East Asian art and culture.[18] The Glasers also traveled extensively throughout the art-historically significant European countries during the 1920s, after the restrictions on mobility imposed by the war were over. In 1923, they undertook a road trip in their own car through "unknown Germany," on which Glaser reported in a four-part series of articles in the *Berliner Börsen-Courier*.[19]

In September 1914, Glaser volunteered for military service, where he first worked in a military hospital in Berlin in 1915 before being sent to the front in Flanders in 1917 as an infantry doctor. He was awarded the "Iron Cross" for this deployment.[20] In civilian life, he bore the title of "Professor," although this was not connected to any office.[21] After the war, he returned to his work at the Kupferstichkabinett, where he was employed as an "assistant" until 1920, when he was finally given a more prestigious post as a curator, which he held until 1924. That it took some ten years for Glaser to be offered this position likely had to do with the interruption of his museum career in the course of the war, but presumably also with anti-Semitic prejudice against Jewish staff members. Elsa Glaser made comments to that effect in Japan in 1911. The fact that her husband had himself baptized as a Protestant in either 1911 or 1914 strongly suggests that he hoped this would improve his career opportunities in the civil service.[22]

By 1912 at the latest, Curt Glaser had begun to oversee the "Neue Abteilung"—the collection of modern and contemporary art—at the Kupferstichkabinett. His excellent social connections as well as his extremely prolific publication activity, in addition to his particular expertise in the field of modern graphic art, made him especially well-suited for this position.[23] During his employment in the Kupferstichkabinett, he wrote his most important scholarly publications. His survey of German painting of the fourteenth through sixteenth centuries was published in 1916, and the monographs on Lucas Cranach the Elder and Hans Holbein the Younger in 1921 and 1924, respectively. Between the two monographs, Glaser produced *Die Graphik der Neuzeit. Vom Anfang des XIX. Jahrhunderts bis zur Gegenwart* (1922), his best-known and also his most comprehensive work, which quickly established itself as the standard text of modern art history and reached a print run of ten thousand copies by the end of the following year.

In October 1924, Curt Glaser became the director of the Kunstbibliothek in Berlin.[24] He was happy to be in a position to turn down the offer to succeed Max Lehrs (1855–1938) as director of the Dresden Kupferstich-Kabinett and stay in Berlin.[25] In the wake of the hyperinflation of 1923, he felt compelled to sell part of his collection.[26] In July 1925, the Glasers moved into an apartment in the building complex at Prinz-Albrecht-Strasse 8, where the art library was also located (p. 71).[27]

In parallel with his work at the Kunstbibliothek, Glaser remained active as an art critic and journalist and undertook extensive trips abroad—for instance, to North Africa in 1930 and to Spain, Greece, and Turkey in 1931—about which he wrote in great detail.[28] In addition, he maintained contact in Europe and the United States with professional colleagues at museums and universities, with collectors and art dealers, and with artists—notably Henri Matisse, Max Beckmann and Ernst Ludwig Kirchner, for whom he advocated in a variety of ways. With Edvard Much in particular—whom he visited numerous times in Oslo and also hosted in his apartment in Berlin (1929)—Glaser developed a special bond that lasted many years and is documented in their correspondence.[29] The portraits of Curt and Elsa produced shortly before World War I by Munch and Matisse also testify to the close contact he nurtured with artists (pp. 81, 144, 145). Glaser's private life was inextricably linked to his professional engagement. Together with his wife, he not only built up their own extensive collection[30] but also acted as an agent and buyer for his father-in-law Hugo Kolker, his mother, and his brother Paul, among others.[31]

THE GREAT UPHEAVAL – 1933

In the early 1930s, Glaser was, as director of the Kunstbibliothek, not only at the height of his career but also in the public eye. There was none other in Berlin's cultural life who combined as many activities and talents in one person as Glaser. According to the magazine *Kunstauktion*, in 1929 he was one of the "most well-known and esteemed personalities in Berlin's artistic life," who as curator had managed the department of modern graphic art at the Kupferstichkabinett in such an "exemplary" way that "today, it can be called the best German collection of graphic art of the nineteenth and twentieth centuries."[32] In the nearly thirty years of his journalistic career, Curt Glaser had written over one thousand articles. He was thus always actively engaged in the latest discussions about exhibitions, architecture, and urban development, as well as Prussian cultural politics. He was a "tone-setting" chronicler, critic, and journalist who took a clear stand on things.[33]

The unexpected death of his wife at the early age of fifty-four on July 10, 1932, caused a sudden break in Glaser's life.[34] Only that spring, the couple had been on a trip together in the United States, where Glaser had given two lectures at the Fogg Art Museum at Harvard University and one in New York.[35] For the couple, making art their own "through traveling, looking, collecting, comparing, discussing, and writing was at the center of Elsa and Curt's married life"[36] and Elsa had been "an invaluable companion ... for her husband," as Glaser's mentor Karl Scheffler wrote.[37] The loss must therefore have been all the more painful. Munch wrote to Glaser about Elsa's death probably around the beginning of 1933: "Dear friend Glaser, You have fallen on hard times. I know what you have lost and what you must be suffering—condolences will do no good .... Well how about coming sometime to Aasgaardstrand? I cannot yet say when exactly. Perhaps it would distract you. With warmest regards your old Edvard Munch / On my wall there is a card from you from America—the dear departed one sends me a nice greeting—as if alive."[38] To honor her memory, on October 18, 1932, Glaser donated Edvard Munch's painting *Music on Karl Johan Street* of 1889 to the Nationalgalerie in Berlin (p. 147).[39] Meanwhile, another drastic change in Glaser's life had already been presaged earlier. In 1931, the Nazi sympathizer Hermann Schmitz (1882–1946), who would later become Glaser's successor as the director of the Kunstbibliothek, accused him in his book on Prussian cultural policy of having obtained his post through favoritism and criticized the assignment of the apartment in the Prinz-Albrecht-Strasse to him as having coming about through good connections to the Prussian cultural administration.[40]

In 1933, the explicit attacks on Glaser became more frequent. On January 11, for instance, the *Völkischer Beobachter* published an article by Wilhelm Pinder (1878–1947) denouncing Adolph Goldschmidt (1864–1944), a Jewish professor of art history at Berlin University. In the article, Goldschmidt was cited as one of the "leading figures" of the Monday salons at Glaser's house and described as "the main culprit for the abuses in the Prussian art administration and especially in the management of the state museums."[41] While the National Socialist author notes that Glaser is "politically neutral," "good-hearted," and free of intrigue, he also explicitly emphasizes—as do many of his colleagues—that Glaser is Jewish.[42]

The events of 1933 that ultimately led to Curt Glaser's dismissal are well known.[43] On February 28, on the pretext of "defense against communist acts of violence threatening the state" as provided in Section 48 of the Weimar Reich Constitution, the "Decree of the Reich President for the Protection of the People and the State" was passed, thereby suspending that same constitution's most important fundamental rights. The decree laid the foundations for the anti-democratic legislation of the Nazi era. With the Reichstag elections of March 5, thanks to a coalition with the ultra-conservative German National People's Party, the National Socialists pushed through the passage of the "Ermächtigungsgesetz" [Enabling Act]—the "Act to Remedy the Distress of the People and the Reich." On March 24, the path to the Nazi dictatorship was cleared and the anti-Semitism of the NSDAP declared state doctrine, giving the Reichskanzler unlimited legislative and executive authority. On April 1, the Reich-wide "Judenboykott" [boycott of Jews] took place—the most extensive boycott of Jewish stores, businesses, medical practices, and law offices to date—which had the specific aim of ousting the Jewish population from economic life.

Only a few days later, on April 7, 1933, the "Law for the Restoration of the Professional Civil Service"[44] was enacted, in anticipation of which Curt Glaser had been placed on temporary leave.[45] A defamatory report titled "Herr Glaser geht in Urlaub" ["Mr. Glaser is going on vacation"] had already appeared in the *Deutsche Zeitung* on April 4 with the cynical claim that Glaser had requested the leave himself.[46] On April 7, press reports confirmed his "leave of absence."[47] This was also noted abroad. On May 9, the *Basler Nachrichten* reported: "As announced, Minister of Culture Rust has placed on leave the director of the State Art Library, Prof. Dr. Curt Glaser, as well as the curator of this library, Dr. Wolfgang Hermann, with immediate effect. Glaser has been active in the German museum service for many years and took over the leadership of the State Art Library after the death of Peter Jessen. He also directed the large exhibitions in the atrium of the neighboring art museum building and organized important lecture series in the library's auditorium. As an author, he is particularly known for his work on Edvard Munch."[48]

The danger of being dismissed due to Jewish origins had already become a frequent topic of discussion in Glaser's professional circles.[49] For instance, Max Sauerlandt (1880–1934), director of the Museum für Kunst und Gewerbe in Hamburg, wrote the following to his wife Alice on March 11, 1933: "In Berlin, on the other hand, word has been given that the museums should keep very quiet on account of the many Jews in leadership positions: Glaser, Friedländer, and so on. They should clad themselves in the protective cloak of invisibility and make as if they do not even exist."[50] The fundamental law of April 7, due to its definition of Jewish descent, was devoted to the restructuring of the entire government bureaucracy in order to ensure its loyalty to the new regime. Two million state and municipal employees were affected—mainly communists and Jews.[51] Glaser had already been forced to vacate his apartment even before his suspension. In April 1933, it became part of the headquarters of the Geheimes Staatspolizeiamt [Secret State Police Service].[52]

On September 27, citing the "Law for the Restoration of the Professional Civil Service," Glaser was definitively dismissed from his post. He would be paid his previous salary for three months following the dismissal and after that, would receive three quarters of his pension.[53]

THE END OF A CAREER: "I HAVE BEEN EXCLUDED FROM EVERYTHING"

On May 9, 1933, Glaser put a large part of his household goods and some works of art up for auction at the Internationales Kunst- und Auktions-Haus Berlin under the title "Collection and Library of a Berlin Art Lover" (pp. 14, 15).[54] On offer were furniture and lighting of the eighteenth century; complete furnishings of the dining, dressing, and bedrooms; sculptures, paintings by old and new masters, oriental and East Asian decorative art, and the precious library. The auction also included other lots from the estates of various collectors.[55] Thus far, the only object that has been documented as not belonging to the Glaser collection is the painting *Landscape with the Flight from Egypt* by a follower of Tobias Verhaecht (1561–1630), which is now in the Hamburger Kunsthalle. It came from the estate of Hanns Emil Fischer (1894–after 1957), a Berlin-based lawyer with whose sister-in-law Curt Glaser was living at the time.[56]

On May 18 and 19, books, drawings, paintings, prints, sculpture, and handicrafts of the sixteenth to twentieth centuries from Glaser's collection were put on the block at Auction No. 180 at Max Perl's in Berlin (p. 32 top).[57] Although his name is not mentioned in the catalogs, even before the auction the provenance was already known not only to insiders such as the art historian Ludwig Burchard (1886–1960) and the director of the Öffentliche Kunstsammlung Basel, Otto Fischer (1886–1948)[58]—attentive readers of the auction announcements would have also known that what was on offer was a large portion of the collection belonging to "the Glasers".[59]

On the second day of the auction, Glaser wrote Munch a letter in which he summed up how his world had "broken down piece by piece" since Elsa's death the previous year and how he had "freed himself from [his] old possessions." "Everything that burdened me had to disappear," he wrote.[60] The word "burden" here certainly has a complex meaning, for he had occupied the apartment and built the collection together with his deceased wife. Parting with this period of his life was therefore an inevitability. It is however difficult to imagine that he would have taken the radical step of completely dissolving his household and collection on such personal grounds alone. The library was the foundation for his work and he certainly would have only been prepared to part with it in the gravest of circumstances (p. 28, bottom). The dissolution of his household and the sale of his property was done with a view to his imminent emigration, the prospect of which he was considering.

Glaser had had the foresight to conduct the auctions at a time when he was still in a position to decide which auction houses he would work with, what he wished to sell, and what he would get to keep in emigration.[61] Moreover, he was able to keep the proceeds of the auction in full, even if they were lower than he had hoped.

Glaser's resolve to make a radical new start was probably also crucially influenced by his new life partner, Maria Milch. As he wrote to Munch on May 19, 1933:[62] "For some time now I have been living again with a woman who is much younger than I am but is very dear to me. I would never have guessed that it could come to this, and I have done nothing to make it so. But I guess I'm not made for being alone, and these days, when it would be especially hard for me to bear the blows of fate without the help and love of another, I'm doubly glad I found the woman."[63] "For some time" could mean about three to four months, and it is thus possible that even before losing the apartment and his post, Glaser had already planned to "downsize" in view of establishing a new household jointly with Maria Milch. However, by the time of his suspension and the loss of the apartment, the external pressures had also come urgently to the fore and compelled the comprehensive sale, which can hardly be compared to a “downsizing” in advance of joining two households.

EMIGRATION

On May 30, Curt Glaser married Maria Milch in Berlin, giving Rauenthaler Strasse 5 in Berlin-Wilmersdorf as his permanent residence.[64] The exact chronology of the events of the following months can be traced only incompletely. In 1962, Maria Glaser reported: “Immediately after the wedding, we drove in our car to Switzerland after a stopover at Lake Starenberg [*sic*]. At first, we did not know where we would stay. Finally, in the second half of 1933, we rented a furnished house in Ronco near Ascona.”[65] This is the address to which Glaser arranged to ship fourteen large boxes of his remaining possessions of furniture, art, and other valuable goods.[66]

On June 7, Glaser’s last article from Berlin appeared in the *Berliner Börsen-Courier*, and on June 13, another one was sent from Nuremberg. It is quite possible that the newlyweds then made the aforementioned stop at Lake Starnberg before going on, either first to Switzerland or directly to Paris. On June 26, Glaser wrote from Paris to Herbert Ihering, editor of the *Berliner Börsen-Courier*, and three more exhibition reports by him from Paris were published on July 5 and 22, and August 2.[67] On July 15, Glaser sent his brother Paul a letter—again, or still —from Paris, instructing him to pick up five paintings that had been on loan from his collection at the Nationalgalerie in Berlin. On July 27, Paul confirmed that he was in possession of the paintings.[68]

By late summer, the Glasers had already arrived in Ticino, as evidenced by a letter dated August 24, 1933, that Glaser sent from Ascona to Berlin to say that he would no longer work for the *Berliner Börsen-Courier*.[69] He wrote on stationary of the Hotel *Monte Verità*. On November 6, 1933, Glaser sent Munch the first lines he had written him since May 19, from Ronco: “Dear old friend! A letter to you has been due for some time, and it will soon be sent. For today, just a greeting from our winter quarters, where I am at least enjoying the sun, after having nothing more to do in Berlin. It is a strange time in which we live.”[70] The postcard shows Glaser with peaked cap and rolled-up white shirt together with his wife Maria on the terrace of an inn (p. 32 bottom).

A month later, on December 9, Glaser wrote to Munch in more detail about his situation, this time again from Paris: “I have been excluded from everything, I am no longer a civil servant and no longer a writer. I am a simple private man who spends his days traveling somewhere in the world, and if I now send you my wishes on your birthday, it is no longer done in the public eye, but privately from one person to another and from friend to friend. Perhaps it is better that way. I have been in the public eye long enough. ... I am now here [in Paris] for a short time ... . For the time being, I am returning to Ronco. I live there with my wife in a small little house high above Lake Maggiore, with a magnificent view, in absolute peace and seclusion from the world. How wonderful life is there, I feel doubly so here in the great hustle and bustle of the big city. We plan to stay there until spring, and I hope to get a bit of work done too. But then I think I shall gradually return to the world, since I do not feel old enough to allow myself to be completely shut out from it. It is not age alone that does it, after all.”[71]

A “SECOND LIFE” IN ASCONA

Glaser’s choice of Ascona was obvious. Around 1900, the town had become a destination attracting adherents of lifestyle reform from all over, and during the two world wars it was a place of refuge for emigrants. On the recommendation of the Russian painter Marianne von Werefkin, the German Baron Eduard von der Heydt (1882–1964) bought Monte Verità, a hill above Ascona, in 1926. As a banker, art collector, and patron of the arts he made it a meeting place for prominent figures from the worlds of art, politics, and society, and he later had good recollections of Curt and Elsa Glaser.[72] The couple had visited him in Ticino in 1928, which is recorded in the guest book.[73]

Glaser’s financial situation in Switzerland is somewhat difficult to grasp, but we can assume that at this early stage he was able to finance his emigration even without the proceeds of the auctions. Moreover, he was not required to pay the Reich Flight Tax until a few years later. Glaser was well off, and this wealth came not only from his marriage to Elsa, but also from his annual income as director of the Art Library of 11,500 reichsmarks per year plus a housing allowance of 1,440 reichsmarks. In addition, he received author’s honoraria of over 3,000 reichsmarks per month.[74] After his dismissal, he continued to receive his salary until the end of 1933, and thereafter, a pension—from which a quarter was deducted because he was Jewish, leaving him just under 5,000 reichsmarks as of 1934. It is impossible to determine in detail how he was able to access his salary and bank deposits from abroad. While the export of currency was already severely restricted, household goods could still be cleared through customs and exported normally in 1933. An important source is the documents of the Wiedergutmachungsamt [Reparations Office] in Berlin. The lawyer Hanns Fischer, who had been married to Maria Glaser’s sister Ellen Milch (1896–1983) since 1926, assisted Glaser with residence permits and financial matters from Berlin as an authorized representative until he emigrated to Brazil in 1939.

At the start of July 1933, Glaser gave official notice of his departure “in the direction of Paris” to Berlin authorities.[75] The couple’s deregistration was put into effect retroactively in March 1934 by the police. During his stay in Switzerland, Glaser kept his official residence at Rauenthaler Strasse 5 in Berlin and received formal permission to stay abroad for the purpose of vacation and research as well as for health and professional reasons. In this way he was able to secure payment of his pension. Perhaps he also hoped the stay abroad would only be temporary. The permit was renewed several times between April 1934 and September 1941,[76] which explains why Maria and Curt Glaser left no trace in the archives, either in Ticino or with the Swiss Fremdenpolizei [immigration police], despite having rented various houses in Ronco and Ascona between 1933 and 1941. Had the couple been living in Switzerland officially as refugees, only a temporary, not an eight-year stay would have been possible, because by the spring of 1933 Switzerland had already introduced a restrictive immigration policy and defined itself as a so-called transit country.[77]

In Ticino, Glaser was under observation by the National Socialists: when the permit for his stay in Switzerland was renewed on September 11, 1935, the responsible agency demanded attestation from the German diplomatic mission stating that "from the German point of view, there were no concerns" regarding Curt Glaser's stay in Switzerland.[78] According to the German Consulate in Lugano, however, this attestation would not be provided because, as the NSDAP local group leader Julius Ammer reported to Berlin, "Curt Glaser moved almost exclusively in Jewish communist emigrant circles. Whereas he was previously living with the protector of Jews Alexander Rapp, he has now moved into the house of one of the fiercest enemies of the new Germany, the Jewish communist architect Schmuklerski, with whom he has a closer friendship. At a recent event in Ascona for the benefit of emigrant children, at which Emil Ludwig read from his works, Dr. Glaser's wife participated as a singer. This also shows that the couple feels closely connected to the emigrats [*sic*]. ... Dr. Glaser receives, without being pecuniarily dependent on it—he is wealthy and should have a good income from his art-historical work on French art—a pension transferred to Switzerland (Mk. 600 or Fr. 600?) Dr. Glaser, however, has only mockery and scorn for this accommodation. For, as I know from reliable sources, he makes fun of the fact that the German authorities so obediently and regularly send him those payments."[79]

Glaser's "second life" in Ascona also brought new joy: on July 22, 1935, his daughter Eva Renate Gertrud was born (p. 17 left). He wrote to Munch to describe "the very vivid symbol of a new and second life, which I accept gratefully, since my first one was shattered."[80] Some family photographs were taken with the little girl when Ellen Fischer—Maria Glaser's sister, who lived in Berlin—visited the new parents in Ticino, presumably in the summer of 1936 (p. 17 right, 158). The portraits suggest that Eva had trisomy 21, also known as Down syndrome, and this has also been recounted in the oral accounts passed down in Maria Milch's family. On September 10, 1938, she was admitted to the La Motta children's nursing home, an anthroposophical institution in Brissago, and by 1940 at the latest, she was in Sonnenhof, a "home for children in need of spiritual care, department of the Clinical Therapeutic Institute" in Arlesheim near Basel. Both homes had been founded by the physician Ita Wegman (1876–1943), a central figure in anthroposophical medicine and a close associate of Rudolf Steiner.[81]

Between 1933 and 1941 Glaser traveled frequently: for instance, several times to Zurich; to Vienna in October 1936; and to Bad Gastein and to Paris in the summer of 1937. Between 1936 and 1939, he also stayed in Florence several times for extended periods to work on a history of the Renaissance. The manuscript, "Materialien zu einer Kunstgeschichte des Quattrocento in Italien" ["Materials for an Art History of the Quattrocento in Italy"] has survived.[82] His colleague Scheffler regarded this as a hopeful attempt "to do significant work after all."[83] In 1934, Glaser had also written Munch about a novel that was neither autobiographical nor a *roman à clef*, but nevertheless based on well-known personalities.[84]

Glaser tried his best to maintain his contacts: for instance, in 1938 he met Max Beckmann in Zurich; in 1935, he renewed contact with Wilhelm Wartmann (1882–1970), the director of the Kunsthaus Zürich; and he visited Robert Musil in his Swiss exile. He frequented the Caffè Verbano, a café in the center of Ascona, newly redesigned by the architect Max Schmuklerski (1905–1995), that was a popular meeting place for recent arrivals.[85] In Florence, he often met with the painter Hans Purrmann (1880–1966), with whom he had long been on friendly terms. The latter had fled to Italy in 1935 due to Nazi persecution and had taken over the honorary post of managing the Villa Romana in Florence. Thanks to him, this institution was a meeting place for art lovers and for artists who had fled Germany.[86]

Glaser's desire to "gradually return to the world" in the spring of 1934 did not come to fruition insofar as he was unable to find new employment. In the summer of 1938, he applied for the position of director of the Öffentliche Kunstsammlung Basel after Otto Fischer prematurely resigned from that post on August 1, 1938. In the list of applicants, Glaser's brief vitae ends with the statement: "Now in Jtalia [*sic*] to study Florentine collections and libraries."[87] He is mentioned as an applicant in the minutes of the Art Commission of September 9, 1938, but the notes also indicate that the hope is to hire someone Swiss.[88] Additionally, one can gather from the record that Jewish candidates would not have garnered a majority of votes either. A letter from the Art Commission of December 15, 1938, to the president of the University of Basel gives the number of applicants (eleven Germans, two French, and ten Swiss), but confirms that although very well-qualified foreign professionals had applied, only the Swiss should be considered because "in the current circumstances, it [would be] generally incomprehensible if the leadership of the largest and most important Swiss art museum were entrusted to a foreigner."[89] In a letter to Hans Purrmann of August 17, 1939, Glaser's friend Karl Scheffler wrote rather casually about Glaser's efforts to find a job: "I fear he has missed the time when he might have found fulfilling work abroad."[90]

TO NEW YORK BY WAY OF HAVANNA

Possibly, Glaser already knew that he would not receive the directorship in Basel when he wrote Munch on December 18, 1938, of his plans to leave for America. But, as he added, it would take time to implement this plan.[91] Some steps to that end are documented in 1940: on March 14, Glaser had the eight paintings (six by Munch, one Heckel and one Kleinschmidt) that he had deposited with the Kunsthaus Zürich transferred to a transport company so they could be shipped to the United States. This plan fell through, however, due to problems with customs.[92]

On October 10, 1940, the New York lawyer Leo S. Gutmann, acting on Glaser's behalf, asked the latter's colleague Paul J. Sachs—a distinguished professor of art history at Harvard University in Cambridge—for a letter of recommendation for Glaser's visa to the United States. To underscore the urgency, he added: "May I add the fact, which is also of importance for the immigration authorities, that Prof. Glaser was dismissed from his job on the first of April 1933, because his conception of art-policy did not agree with the new art-principles of the Nazi regime. If Switzerland should come under the influence of Germany or the Nazi sympathizers, Dr. Curt Glaser would be placed in a very dangerous position. It would probably be helpful if this fact could be mentioned too."[93] Five days later, Sachs sent Gutmann the needed recommendation, thus contributing critically to securing the immigration permit.[94]

Curt and Maria Glaser, meanwhile, also had to worry about the future of their daughter Eva, who was now in care in Arlesheim. It was difficult for physically and mentally impaired people to emigrate to the United States due to restrictive entry requirements, but above all, the long sea voyage with an extended stay in Cuba would likely not have been advisable given her health condition.[95] On November 18, Maria Glaser made a spontaneous visit to her daughter and mentioned the impending move to Zurich as well as her husband's plans to move to the United States as soon as possible. She announced another visit in December.[96] On November 22, Ita Wegman inquired about securing the payments,[97] and Curt Glaser answered on November 25 from Ascona: "Obviously, in the event our plans for America should still come to fruition, which seems very doubtful, I have given thought to financing Eva's continued stay in your care and have already taken measures that will in any case secure the monthly payments. But it is equally obvious that we would not leave without coming to Arlesheim first to say goodbye and to discuss whatever is necessary."[98]

Meanwhile, Glaser was also looking to solve the problem of the paintings he had deposited at the Kunsthaus Zürich. In a letter to its director, Wilhelm Wartmann, dated December 9, 1940, he sounded distraught over the fact that the painting *Music on Karl Johan Street* by Munch, which was so dear to him, could not be sent to the United States (p. 147).[99] He had demanded the painting back from the Nationalgalerie in Berlin due to noncompliance with the conditions of the gift and had it brought to Switzerland.[100] As to his own situation, he concluded: "Whether I will be able to leave Europe myself remains to be seen. I doubt very much that it will be possible. But the pictures will have to stay here, one way or another. In one of your letters, you expressed your regret that they should be lost to Europe. I now place the fate of the paintings in your hands."[101] The painting, which he had given to the Nationalgalerie in 1932 in memory of his first wife, Elsa, and did not bring to Zurich until 1939, was purchased by the Kunsthaus. It seems to have been particularly important to him, for he was also relieved to avoid the risk of the possible loss during shipment of "such an important, irreplaceable work of art" and considered himself fortunate that "the painting could find a permanent place in your collection."[102] Glaser left the other six works as a deposit at the Kunsthaus in order to "fulfill any pecuniary obligations in Switzerland," by which he surely meant the costs of their daughter's care in Arlesheim.[103]

On January 2, 1941, Glaser wrote to announce his departure to Max J. Friedländer (1867–1958). On January 14, the former colleague—who had also been dismissed from his post as director of the Staatliche Gemäldegalerie Berlin and had fled to the Netherlands in 1939—wrote back to him from The Hague: "Your card of Jan. 2 made me very happy .... So you too are on the move. Hopefully this greeting will still reach you—with my wishes that your hopes will be fulfilled."[104]

On February 26, 1941, the Glasers said goodbye to their daughter in Arlesheim. Wegman reported to Werner Pache, the director of the home: "On Wednesday, Mr. and Mrs. Prof. Glaser will come to Arlesheim to visit Eva Renate. I was at the concert given for their farewell. They were also here for a music evening once. They were quite friendly and much more open than they had ever been, and it then became clear to me, also because the woman said so, that she had actually expected me to have invited her to sing at the Casa, and when this did not happen, she believed that we did not want to have anything to do with them. It made me very sorry, because I could feel how these people were always reading something into everything because of the current attitudes toward the Jews.—They were quite pleased that Miss Eisenmenger [the specialist caregiver] will stay with Eva Renate, and they have the greatest confidence in us, so I have the feeling that we would all be on good terms with one another, if you were also to extend a welcome. I heard that they do have money, and perhaps it would be possible to get an advance payment for Eva Renate. I was also pleased to hear that Miss Eisenmenger is staying. It would have been quite hard for the Glasers if they had left knowing that the child would have to stay behind without Miss Eisenmenger."[105]

The forms for the "Ueberseeische Auswanderung im Jahre 1941" [Immigration Overseas in 1941] record that they were both retired and last resided in Ascona. Their departure from Switzerland was given as February 1941, on the steamer Magallanes, bound for Havana from the port in Vigo on the northwest coast of Spain. Their travel status was "émigrant/e" and the all-inclusive fare per person was CHF 1643.20 (pp. 34, 36). The stamp on the 1941 documents is proof that the Glasers had goods being shipped with them into exile. Without proof of assets, the interim stay in Cuba would not have been possible.[106]

The Glasers arrived in New York from Havana on May 13 on the SS Monterey (pp. 35, 37), as indicated in an affidavit dated October 16, 1941. Shortly before this, the payment of Glaser's pension from Berlin had ceased with the expiration of the term period on September 30, 1941, and on November 30, 1941, he also lost his German citizenship in accordance with the 11th decree of the Reich Citizenship Law.[107] Nonetheless, according to Strobl, during the time of their exile, the Glasers were described as "wealthy."[108] Glaser was also apparently looking for a job in New York, despite the tuberculosis that already plagued him.[109] This can be surmised from a letter of January 11, 1942 that Goldschmidt wrote to Glaser: "You are in a good position, in that you would be able to make a nice home for yourself there without relying on others, and will be able to work well there. After all, you have four good libraries at your disposal."[110] Goldschmidt encouraged him and gave him various suggestions for professional contacts, although he added it is difficult for immigrants to find a job in teaching; he also suggested Glaser would be well-suited for a "museum position."

But Glaser did not succeed in regaining a foothold professionally in the United States either, although he was only in his early sixties. On February 23, 1943, his daughter died of "cardiac paralysis" at the age of seven and a half.[111] His own illness had meanwhile progressed as well, and he died that same year on November 23 at the hospital in Lake Placid, New York, at the age of sixty-four.[112]

Of the works of art remaining to him, Glaser seems to have brought only drawings with him to the United States.[113] It was not until after Glaser's death that his widow had two of the Munch works that had been stored in Zurich picked up by his trustee and art dealer Charles Albert de Burlet (1882–1956) on March 14, 1947, and deposited at the Kunstmuseum Basel.[114] Glaser was apparently also able to save two more paintings in Switzerland: Max Beckmann's *Self-Portrait with Saxophone* (p. 87) and his *Portrait of Curt Glaser* (p. 6). Their whereabouts are, however, unknown up to the time his widow had them sold by the art dealer Walter Feilchenfeldt in Zurich in 1954 and 1958, respectively. Possibly they had been deposited there for some time.[115]

On October 6, 1947, Purrmann reported in a letter to Scheffler that he had met Maria Glaser—who was running a bookstore in New York—in Ticino: "I found it sad that one could only speak of her husband in memory. There is hardly a person I would have liked to see again as much as him."[116]

1 *The New York Times*, November 25, 1943, p. 26.
This essay is based largely on the historical facts as presented in 2018 by the Kunstmuseum Basel in its report: *Entscheid der Kunstkommission in Sachen Curt Glaser*, of November 21, 2018, available at kunstmuseumbasel.ch/curtglaser, cited in the following as Entscheid Basel 2018.
A condensed version of the report in English is also available on the English-language website, but not all the material from the Entscheid referenced in this essay is contained therein.
2 Walravens 1990a, Walravens 1990b; see also Walravens 2012.
3 Strobl 2006; further, see Strobl 2012.
4 Brand/Schulze Altcappenberg 2014.
5 Entscheid Basel 2018.
6 When no further citation is given, biographical details are taken from Strobl 2006 and Brand/Schulze Altcappenberg 2014.
7 Paul's application for entry to Liechtenstein was rejected in 1939 (Fürstentum Liechtenstein, Amt für Kultur, Landesarchiv, LI LA RF 184/270/001 and LI LA RF 184/270/004; e-archiv.li/textDetail.aspx?backurl=editionSuche.aspx?eid=1&etID=41920&eID=1).
8 Brand/Schulze Altcappenberg 2014, p. 370.
9 For Elsa's biography and her role in Glaser's life, see the essay by Lynn Rother and Max Koss.
10 Brand/Schulze Altcappenberg 2014, p. 370, stress Elsa Glaser's central role in this context; see also the Entscheid Basel 2018, p. 11–12, as well as the essay by Lynn Rother and Max Koss, pp. 16, 17.
11 Entscheid Basel 2018, p. 114. On the Glaser collection, see the essay by Judith Rauser.
12 Strobl 2006, p. 12.
13 Ibid., p. 13. Glaser was active as the publisher of the supplement, together with Gustav Kirstein and Hans Tietze, until March 1926, when it was merged back into the *Zeitschrift für bildende Kunst* for financial reasons.
14 Ibid., p. 15. The first volume appeared in 1920.
15 Glaser 1908.
16 Entscheid Basel 2018, p. 13; also see the essay by Andreas Schalhorn in the German volume, pp. 49–50.
17 Curt Glaser, "Claude Monet," *Hamburgischer Correspondent*, no. 119, December 3, 1903.
18 Brand/Schulze Altcappenberg 2014, p. 372; also see Strobl 2006, pp. 70–81 and Kuwabara 2012.
19 Strobl 2006, p. 25.
20 Brand/Schulze Altcappenberg 2014, p. 382.
21 *Kunstchronik*, NF 28, 1916/1917, no. 43, col. 519.
22 Brand/Schulze Altcappenberg 2014, p. 373; see also the quotation from Elsa Glaser in Kuwabara 2012, p. 84. It is not known whether Elsa also converted.
23 Brand/Schulze Altcappenberg 2014, p. 382; see also the essay by Andreas Schalhorn in the German volume.
24 For more detail, see the essay by Joachim Brand in the German volume.
25 Curt Glaser to Edvard Munch, November 10, 1923, Munchmuseet, Oslo, MM K 2346.
26 Ibid.: "I am no longer in a position to maintain our art collection in its entirety. So, a few things have changed in the apartment."
27 The dwelling in question was not a civil service apartment that Glaser was automatically entitled to rent as the director of the Kunstbibliothek. Cf. Entscheid Basel 2018, pp. 31–40. This "residential wing" was also known as the "Professorenanbau" [professors annex]. With great thanks to Ulrich Tempel, Berlin, for this information. See also Topographie des Terrors 2008, pp. 8–27.
28 On his travel accounts, see Strobl 2006, pp. 95–97.
29 For more on this, see the essay by Joachim Sieber in the German volume.
30 On the Glasers' private collection, see Strobl 2006, pp. 22–26, and the essay by Judith Rauser.
31 Curt Glaser to Edvard Munch, September 7, 1913, Munchmuseet, Oslo, MM K 2270.
32 "Personalien: Curt Glaser," in: *Die Kunstauktion: Deutsches Nachrichtenblatt des gesamten Kunstmarktes und Buchmarktes* 3, no. 22 (June 2, 1929), p. 12.
33 Brand/Schulze Altcappenberg 2014, p. 375. Glaser's extensive list of publications is compiled in Strobl 2006, pp. 236–84.
34 On the cause of her death, see the essay by Lynn Rother and Max Koss, p. 19, note 19.
35 *Bulletin of the Fogg Art Museum* 1, no. 4 (May 1932), p. 78. The travel accounts from this trip appeared in book form under the title *Amerika baut auf!* (Berlin, 1932).
36 Brand/Schulze Altcappenberg 2014, p. 470.
37 Scheffler 1946, p. 218.
38 Edvard Munch to Curt Glaser [1933?], Munchmuseet, Oslo, MM K 2244.
39 On the further history of the painting, see the essay by Joachim Sieber in the German volume, pp. 138–40.
40 Schmitz 1931, pp. 164–65.
41 Quoted in Entscheid Basel 2018, p. 41.
42 Ibid., p. 42.
43 Entscheid Basel 2018, pp. 19–24; Walk 1981, Friedländer 1998.
44 Walk 1981, p. 12.
45 For documentation, see Entscheid Basel 2018, p. 24, esp. note 100.
46 "Herr Glaser geht in Urlaub," *Deutsche Zeitung*, no. 80, April 4, 1933.
47 Entscheid Basel 2018, p. 26.
48 *Basler Nachrichten* 89, no. 126 (1933).
49 For more on the topic of art historians in exile, see Wendland 1998.
50 Sauerlandt 1957, p. 415.
51 Friedländer 1998, p. 40.
52 Ibid., p. 31–40; see also the essay by Joachim Brand in the German volume, p. 73.
53 Entscheid Basel 2018, pp. 27–28.
54 Ausst.-Kat. Berlin 1933a.
55 Entscheid Basel 2018, p. 43.
56 On the restitution and repurchase of the painting by the Hamburger Kunsthalle, see the report of the Hamburger Behörde für Kultur und Medien of July 30, 2018; hamburg.de/pressearchiv-fhh/11449606/restitution-landschaftsgemaelde-rueckkauf-kunsthalle/.
57 Aukt.-Kat. Berlin 1933b.
58 See the essay by Anita Haldemann, p. 26.
59 Entscheid Basel 2018, pp. 46–47, 50.
60 Curt Glaser to Edvard Munch, May 19, 1933, Munchmuseet, Oslo, MM K 2387.
61 On the purchase of 200 works by the Öffentliche Kunstsammlung Basel see the essay by Anita Haldemann.
62 For more on this, see also the essay by Lynn Rother und Max Koss, p. 17.
63 Curt Glaser to Edvard Munch, May 19, 1933, Munchmuseet, Oslo, MM K 2387.
64 Entscheid Basel 2018, p. 39, esp. note 184.
65 This report was made in the form of an affidavit during the compensation proceedings for Nazi persecution-related losses. See Entscheid Basel 2018, p. 89 with note 466.
66 Ibid., p. 83.
67 Ibid., pp. 86–87.
68 Ibid., pp. 87–88 with note 459.
69 Curt Glaser to Herbert Ihering, of the *Berliner Börsen-Courier*, August 24, 1933, archive of the Akademie der Bildenden Künste Berlin, shelf mark Ihering 1336: "After considerable reflection, it seems to me best if I retire from reporting on art regularly. I foresee that I would find myself in a constant serious conflict of conscience. … As a dismissed civil servant and a Jew, I would be in a very precarious situation."
70 Curt Glaser to Edvard Munch, November 6, 1933, Munchmuseet, Oslo, MM K 2388.
71 Curt Glaser to Edvard Munch, December 9, 1933, Munchmuseet, Oslo, MM K 2389.
72 Von der Heydt/von Rheinbaben 1958, p. 74: "I can name the well-known Curt Glaser and his first wife Elsa, who played a big role in Berlin artistic circles and often hosted interesting gatherings where you could meet all manner of artistically interesting sorts in good combination."
73 Curt Glaser, "Reise im Auto. III: Von Basel über die Alpenpässe nach dem Süden," *Berliner Börsen-Courier*, no. 443, September 21, 1928, and "Ascona," *Berliner Börsen-Courier*, no. 447, September 23, 1928; see also Ausst.-Kat. Zürich, pp. 242–43.
74 For details regarding Glaser's financial situation, pension, and compensation claims, see Entscheid Basel 2018, pp. 94–107.
75 Quoted in Strobl 2006, p. 19, note 32.
76 For details and sources, see Entscheid Basel 2018, pp. 104–05.
77 Unabhängige Expertenkommission Schweiz–Zweiter Weltkrieg 2001, p. 283, and Entscheid Basel 2018, pp. 90–91.
78 Quoted in Entscheid Basel 2018, p. 101.
79 Ibid., pp. 101–02.
80 Curt Glaser to Edvard Munch, July 22, 1935, Munchmuseet, Oslo, MM K 2391.
81 See Entscheid Basel 2018, pp. 93–94.
82 Reprinted in Walravens 2012, pp. 85–387.
83 Karl Scheffler to Hans Purrmann, May 6, 1940, quoted in Billeter/Kennedy/Matelowski 2021, p. 100.
84 Curt Glaser to Edvard Munch, December 10, 1934, Munchmuseet, Oslo, MM K 2390.
85 On Schmuklerski, see archiv.gta.arch.ethz.ch/nachlaesse-vorlaesse/max-schmuklerski-19051995.
86 On the Villa Romana, see Ausst.-Kat. Bonn 2013.
87 Kunstmuseum Basel, archive, G12-02_1938.
88 Minutes of the Meeting of the Kunstkommission from September 9, 1938, Kunstmuseum Basel, archive, B1/16-Protokolle der Kunstkommission, pp. 134–35; see also Entscheid Basel 2018, pp. 129–30.
89 Letter from the Kommission concerning the Öffentliche Sammlung to the president of the Universität Basel, Prof. Dr. M. Gerwig, December 15, 1938, Kunstmuseum Basel, archive, E07-03.
90 Billeter/Kennedy/Matelowski 2021, p. 90.
91 Curt Glaser to Edvard Munch, December 18, 1938, Munchmuseet, Oslo, MM K 2394.
92 See the essay by Joachim Sieber in the German volume, pp. 138–39.
93 Leo S. Gutmann to Paul J. Sachs, October 10, 1940. Paul J. Sachs Papers (HC 3), folder 724. Harvard Art Museums Archives, Harvard University, Cambridge, MA.

94 Paul J. Sachs to Leo S. Gutmann, October 15, 1940, ibid.
95 Irmo Marini and Mark A. Stenicki, eds., *Psychological and Social Impact of Illness and Disability* (New York, 2017), pp. 3–13. A weight curve chart of children in "Sonnenhof" from September 1940 through May 1941 shows that Eva's weight was very low. See archive, Ita Wegman Institut, archive Sonnenhof, Arlesheim. She died two years later of cardiac paralysis, see note 112.
96 Werner Pache (director of the "Sonnenhof") to Ita Wegman, November 18, 1940: "Mrs. Glaser suddenly turned up here unannounced and looked in on Evchen but did not want anyone of us to be fetched. She told Miss Eisenmenger en passant that they would soon be moving to Zurich and that her husband wanted to go to America as soon as possible, if they could only arrange it. Of course they thought they would leave Evchen here, since she was in good hands; she would come again in December.
It would, in our view, be of course necessary to discuss Evchen's situation with her parents before their possible departure. Otherwise there could be financial and other difficulties. However, the Glasers are honorable people and I think that they will have already thought about the fact that Evchen's future must be secured. Would it be possible for you to have a talk with the Glasers before they leave Ascona?" Archive, Ita Wegman Institut, archive Sonnenhof, Arlesheim. With great thanks to Tessa Rosebrock for indexing this source and to Gunhild Pörksen and Niklaus Hottinger for obtaining the archival material.
97 Ita Wegman to Curt Glaser, November 22, 1940, archive, Ita Wegman Institut, archive Sonnenhof, Arlesheim.
98 Curt Glaser to Ita Wegman, November 25, 1940, ibid.
99 Curt Glaser to Wilhelm Wartmann, December 9, 1940, archive Zürcher Kunstgesellschaft/Kunsthaus Zürich, incoming correspondence archive 10.30.30.067; see also the essay by Joachim Sieber in the German volume, pp. 139–40.
100 See the essay by Joachim Sieber in the German volume, pp. 138–39.
101 Ibid.
102 Curt Glaser to Wilhelm Wartmann, December 12, 1940, archive Zürcher Kunstgesellschaft/Kunsthaus Zürich, incoming correspondence archive 10.30.30.067.
103 Ibid.
104 Max J. Friedländer to Curt Glaser (Ascona), January 14, 1941, quoted in Walravens 1990a, pp. 111–12 (original at the Leo Baeck Institute, New York).
105 Ita Wegman to Werner Pache (Ascona), February 8, 1941, archive, Ita Wegman Institut, archive Sonnenhof, Arlesheim.
106 With thanks to Tessa Rosebrock for this information; see Krohn 1998, and Heimat und Exil 2006.
107 Ibid., note 574.
108 Strobl 2006, p. 21.
109 On Glaser's life in exile in the United States, see the essay by Jennifer Tonkovich, p. 33.
110 Adolph Goldschmidt (Basel) to Curt Glaser (New York), January 11, 1942, quoted in Walravens 1990a, pp. 109–10 (original at the Leo Baeck Institute, New York).
111 Entry in the records of the "Sonnenhof", archive, Ita Wegman Institut, archive Sonnenhof, Arlesheim. Strobl 2006, p. 20, including note 40, gives the date of death as February 10, 1935, which probably comes from a mistake in the records of the compensation proceedings; see Entscheid Basel 2018, p. 93, note 500.
112 Strobl 2006, pp. 20–21.
113 See the essay by Jennifer Tonkovich, p. 33.
114 Kunstmuseum Basel, archive, account book, entry from August 23, 1947, "Depositum von Frau Maria Glaser, 27 West 96th St. New York 25, N.Y[.]"; see Entscheid Basel 2018, pp. 122–23.
115 Information personally provided by Walter Feilchenfeldt, May 15, 2018.
116 Hans Purrmann to Karl Scheffler, October 10, 1947, cf. Billeter/Kennedy/Matelowski 2021, p. 133.

Lynn Rother
Max Koss

"OH, YOU ARE A SCIENTIST!" ELSA GLASER AND ART HISTORY

In October 1932, a few months after Elsa Glaser's untimely death at the age of fifty-four, her widower Curt donated a painting from their art collection, Edvard Munch's *Music on Karl Johan Street* (p. 147), to the Nationalgalerie in Berlin. He stipulated that the painting should be shown permanently alongside a plaque commemorating his beloved wife.[1] This commemoration has been eroded over time by institutions.[2] The gradual disappearance of Elsa, who was for Curt not just a wife but an intellectual partner for almost thirty years, leaves us with only fragments of her life. While she is there in the literature and media coverage that has since emerged about Curt Glaser—as not only an art historian and collector, but also as a victim of National Socialist persecution—it is in passing mentions and, indeed, the footnotes. Elsa has become almost forgettable, even though her contemporaries saw in her a remarkable personality.

In his intellectual biography of Curt Glaser, Andreas Strobl writes the following about Elsa, whose life and legacy are the subject of this essay: "We have no way to ascertain how much she supported Curt Glaser in his work."[3] It is true that the archival and documentary record relating to Elsa Glaser is patchy, with little to no evidence and few highlights, which complicates the task of describing with certainty who Elsa Glaser was and what her legacy might be, especially in regard to her intellectual work. The statement seems to imply that if further evidence came to light, it would show Elsa in a supporting role to her husband's career. It thus echoes a gendered separation of work and life. Such an assumption is at odds with the imbricated relationship Elsa and Curt Glaser seem to have had in most aspects of life, including work, which others have previously acknowledged and which can be glimpsed from Edvard Munch's 1913 double portrait of the couple (p. 145).[4] Indeed, the life Elsa and Curt Glaser chose for themselves—one thoroughly dedicated to art in all its various aspects—ought to be examined as a collaborative endeavor of world-making. The Glaser cosmos rotated upon two axes: Curt *and* Elsa Glaser.

This essay proposes a holistic view of Elsa Glaser's life, looking at known, but also new archival and documentary sources. Even though Elsa's life and her activities were deeply enmeshed with that of her husband's, our emphasis is on Elsa's agency, including her role, particularly in the second half of the 1920s, in helping to make the Glasers' residence a prominent, yet exclusive hub for a selection of Berlin's cultured elite. Agency extends further though, beyond such traditionally gendered duties, to include her intellectual contributions to art history, which are harder to pin down. Piecing together a fuller picture of her necessitates that we read the existing scholarship on her husband, with the view to disentangling the narrative of Elsa's life from that of his.

While the acts of drawing out individual agency and stressing imbricated lives may seem like something of a contradiction, we see them as two sides of the same coin. A recovery or reconstruction of female agency operates against the background of geographically diverse and diachronically evolving legal restrictions on women's rights, in particular the right to own.[5] In the case of Jewish women, the space in which they were able to operate was even more restricted, both in terms of the rules of patriarchy and widespread anti-Semitic resentment.[6] Elsa Glaser was, as will become clear, well aware of these limitations. Perhaps, for her, working towards societal acceptance in a patriarchal system meant making sure that her husband's career as an intellectual flourished?

Reconstructing Elsa's agency and spirit by revisiting footnotes and archival sources allows us to remember her as a modern woman who was all about living life to the fullest.

THE EARLY YEARS: BLISS

Elsa Kolker was born in Breslau, Silesia, then part of the German Empire, on May 7, 1878, as the daughter of Renate "Natalie" Kolker (1852–1921), née Glaser, and the industrialist and art collector Hugo Kolker (1845–1915), who had achieved prosperity through an oil refinery, a chemical plant, and a range of associated ventures.[7] When she married her cousin Curt Glaser in her city of birth on August 12, 1903, at the age of twenty-five, the marriage record noted, unsurprisingly for a woman of her standing, that she was without profession.[8] Her upbringing among the wealthy Jewish bourgeoisie would have made her an educated young woman without a realistic professional path laid out for her, especially during a time when female students were still not allowed to enroll full-time in a majority of disciplines in German universities.[9]

Given that Elsa's material needs were catered for, thanks to her family's successful business interests, she turned her intellectual curiosity to whatever her heart desired. Curt had just finished his doctorate in medicine in 1902 and, with the financial support of Elsa's family, was able to commit to further study in the field of art history, obtaining a doctorate in 1907 under the supervision of Heinrich Wölfflin. It has been suggested that it was Elsa who brought him to the path of art history in the first place.[10] This is plausible insofar as she had, as the paternal cousin of Curt, ample time and opportunity to share her own interests with him before their marriage, nudging him ever closer to pursuing a career in art history, however financially insecure it may have been.

As far as the surviving testimony allows us an evaluation of the Glasers' marriage, it was not only a mutually beneficial one, but also seems to have been filled with happiness and intimacy—all in the pursuit of art, art-historical knowledge, and a social life centered around intellectuals and artists, not just in Berlin, but in other parts of the world as well. And while the Glasers did not have any children, whether by choice or fate, this gave them the liberty to travel and explore the world to their heart's content.[11]

Indeed, their extensive traveling, which would continue up until Elsa's death, formed a crucial aspect of their marriage. Their voyage to Japan in 1911 provides an illuminating glimpse into what their life was like before World War I broke out, during the very last years of the long nineteenth century. Mokutarô Kinoshita's account of the Glasers' visits to a number of private Japanese art collections gives a vivid description of Elsa Glaser's personality, foregrounding her intellectual curiosity, but also the fact that she continually impressed her local hosts not only with her Japanese language skills, but also with her in-depth knowledge of Japanese art and cultural history, including the intricacies of Japanese tea ceremonies.[12] This led one of the hosts to observe: "Oh, you are a scientist!"[13]

What becomes apparent in the text is the author's admiration for the couple's independent spirit, their curiosity, and their willingness to intellectually work through the experiences they shared in Japan. In this regard, it is telling that Kinoshita relayed Elsa's complaint about the sociocultural and professional barriers that she and her husband faced at home as non-Christians, emphasizing the paradoxical point that *because* they were strangers to each other, they could engage in a prejudice-free, cross-cultural conversation.[14] Already in 1911, then, we have indications that for Elsa and Curt Glaser creating spaces of conversation as places for both socializing and as mutual understanding was an essential component of their shared intellectual practice.[15]

The Glasers' interest in Edvard Munch can be dated to 1910;[16] three years later, when their Munch collection was already considered to be the outstanding one in Germany,[17] they encountered one another personally for the first time: the Glasers travelled to Norway to visit Edvard Munch; while there, he painted two portraits of Elsa. The couple would also function as intermediaries between Munch and Hugo Kolker, who, with their help, had also begun amassing an art collection. The couple's visit to Norway is documented, for example, in a photograph showing them sitting together with Munch and a number of other figures in a large automobile (pp. 22, 26). Not only is Elsa the only woman in the group, but she is also seen next to Munch at the back of the car, towering over the others.

The two near-identical portrait paintings of Elsa by Munch produced on this occasion show Elsa in a seated and equally alert posture (p. 144). Here, she appears somewhat suspended between the formality of the portrait pose and her inquiring and rule-bending spirit. Her body barely fits within the picture's limits, brushing the edges with her right elbow and feet. The tension and alertness expressed through arrangement and posture are further underlined by the sitter's gaze, directly addressing the viewer. Her head and face are the most articulated elements of the image. They are also presented bust-like, through the off-setting color accents provided by the orange shoulder elements of her otherwise simple but elegant purple dress. Around the figure, the picture is dominated by blotchiness, indistinct contours, and a certain lack of form. It is not possible, for example, to determine whether the image shows an interior or an exterior space, and the light-colored rectangle by Elsa's left arm may be an opening, a mirror, or an artwork. This indeterminacy of the surroundings makes Elsa's presence all the more commanding.

Her spirit and intelligence shine through in an equally poignant portrait that Henri Matisse drew of her in June 1914 during a visit of the Glasers to Paris, mere weeks before Europe plunged into war and the shared life of the Glasers entered a new phase (p. 81). The elegant graphite drawing of Elsa's face, framed by her stylish haircut, picks up the directness of the Munch portraits. In a frontal pose, Elsa's vitality is captured through her eyes, which are the darkest and most pronounced feature of the drawing. At the same time, the abstracting qualities of the drawing create a certain distance with the viewer, giving it an air of aloofness. The Matisse drawing and a photograph of Elsa from 1915, captured in a fashionable outfit and holding her small dog, resurface towards the end of Elsa's life in 1930. They were shown in the exhibition "Gezeichnet oder geknipst" ["Drawn or Snapped"], organized by the art critic and publisher Paul Westheim at the Reckendorf publishing house. Her two portraits were then published side by side by Westheim in *Das Kunstblatt* (p. 25), a leading art periodical of the Weimar Republic.[18]

The moment of creation of the Matisse drawing marked a high point of Elsa and Curt Glaser's shared adventures, as well as something of an epochal caesura. Its prominent re-appearance and distribution fifteen years later can be seen as a kind of a punctuation mark in the final phase of Elsa's life, as well as a reminder of the person she used to be in happier times.

THE LATER YEARS: AN OPEN HOUSE

The years following World War I and up until Elsa's premature death in 1932 were marked both by continuities and disruptions.[19] This period saw the steady progress of Elsa's husband's career, who, after being promoted to a curatorial position at Berlin's Kupferstichkabinett in 1920, became the director of the Kunstbibliothek (Art Library) in 1924.[20] Against this slow unfolding of a successful professional career, an increasing number of difficult moments came into relief, including financial difficulties due to the economic upheavals of the 1920s, not least Germany's inflation, which lasted until 1923, and Elsa's growing impairments.[21]

Indeed, one significant aspect of Elsa's life, and one that her contemporaries reacted to in a variety of ways, were her growing physical ailments, the consequences of which can be glimpsed in another drawn double portrait of the Glasers by Munch, showing Elsa visibly weary (p. 43 left).[22] Elsa's hearing difficulties—signs of which were recorded even before the war—grew more acute with the years, and we see them reflected in the perceptions and writings of those around her.[23] When Kinoshita, their trusted guide and friend from Japan, visited the couple in the fall of 1922, he recognized both the financial difficulties of the couple as well as Elsa's deteriorating health.[24] In a letter from 1965, Mathilde "Quappi" Beckmann, Max Beckmann's widow, remembered meeting Elsa around 1928, when her health was markedly on the decline: "The poor lady was almost deaf when I knew her, and she was wearing those horrible hearing-aids from that time, holding a receiver box in front of her, as she constantly interrupted her husband when sitting at the dining table talking to Max with 'Was hat er gesagt?' ['What did he say?'] in a sharp loud voice. I remember her as very intelligent but it was always an embarrassing pathetic situation at the dinner table, as if she was engulfed by constant suspicion."[25]

This stands in contrast to the assessment by Karl Scheffler, friend and mentor to the Glasers, who wrote that despite having to use her "apparatus," she was "free of the kinds of suspicion usually associated with this plight."[26] Nevertheless, in his eulogy for Elsa (p. 43 right), Scheffler also acknowledged her mercurial personality, "oscillating between deep melancholy and sudden highs," while praising her passionate opinions, her disregard for conventions, her brilliance and intelligence, and her sheer endless enthusiasm. Her remarkable personality led him to conclude that, for those that knew her, she would be "unforgettable."[27]

Her precarious health situation notwithstanding, the second half of the 1920s saw Elsa take on an important role in the social fabric of Berlin's cultured elite. While the ever curious Elsa generally practiced an open house policy, her previously sporadic hospitality took a more formal and thus a more publicly assertive turn with the regular Monday evening receptions that the Glasers began to hold at their spacious, art- and book-filled residence. The apartment was but one of the perks of Elsa's husband's position as the director of the Kunstbibliothek.[28] Since he did not take up this position until 1924 and they only moved in July 1925, the gatherings only lasted for a relatively short period of time. Even so, they quickly became a Berlin fixture, if a somewhat exclusive one, and garnered attention not only in the capital, but also beyond. Their prominence can be glimpsed from an article on one of the gatherings in the *Weltspiegel* supplement of one of Germany's leading liberal newspapers at the time, the *Berliner Tageblatt*, written by the critic and still rare female PhDs of the time, Dr. Augusta von Oertzen. The evening was photographed by Käte Witkower, sister of the art historian Rudolf Witkower. Von Oertzen opens the text stressing how "lucky" one should count oneself to be included in the gatherings (p. 30).[29]

That Elsa and Curt Glaser, the world-savvy travelers and collectors of both art and friendships, would make a point of curating the guest list comes as no surprise.[30] Indeed, a deeper consideration of how the Glasers wanted the gatherings to be seen can provide another perspective on their self-fashioning, as well as the potential sociocultural lineages they sought to align themselves with. In one of the photographs accompanying the article, we can see the couples Else and Bruno Cassirer and Dora and Karl Scheffler, as well as the painters Hans Purrmann and Rudolf Grossmann, sitting around a table in the residence's intimate salon.[31] Prominently displayed behind them, among a selection of ethnographic sculptures, we see Edvard Munch's large-scale *Music on Karl Johan Street* (p. 147), the rare and early painting that Curt Glaser later donated to Berlin's Nationalgalerie in honor of Elsa. It is a snapshot-like image of a street scene, with a brass band playing, and various people going about their business, barely listening to the music. It is a somewhat incongruous, intellectually challenging image, with the imagined music of the band being undercut by a large swath of empty street, a puddle's reflection, and people caught somewhere between attention and distraction.

The public at the Glaser house, on the other hand, usually came together after the lecture series Curt Glaser had established at the Kunstbibliothek. It was thus both varied and exclusive, including museum professionals and writers, such as Robert Musil, as well as artists like Max Beckmann. With the publisher Bruno Cassirer present—who in 1898 had opened one of the city's first and most important galleries and publishing ventures for modern art with his cousin Paul—and with Munch's paintings on the walls, the genealogy of these gatherings harkens back to the beginnings of modern art in Berlin in the early to mid-1890s. Munch was then part of the city's bohème around the Swedish playwright August Strindberg and the circle known as the "Schwarzes Ferkel" (Black Piglet).[32] Having Elsa's 1913 portrait by Munch on view in the salon would not only have functioned as a reminder of these beginnings, but it would have also made the personal and spiritual connections of the Glasers to them palpable.

This earlier moment of artistic modernism in Berlin was also the moment of the famous salon of Cornelie Richter (1842–1922). The young Richter converted from Judaism to Protestantism, as Curt Glaser would also later do to boost his standing in the professional museum world.[33] By the time the Glasers began their own formal evening gatherings decades later, hospitality and salons, with their spirit of the long nineteenth century, as they were also practiced in Jewish households, were alive but waning.[34] This tradition had begun around 1800, with the gatherings at the residence of Rahel Varnhagen von Ense (1771–1833) or Henriette Hertz (1764–1847). Among the contemporaries of the Glasers, it was Marianne Goldschmidt-Rothschild (1892–1973), one of the richest women in Germany living at Pariser Platz, who held salons attracting financiers, courtiers, diplomats, and intellectuals, as well as extravagant dance parties, extending long into the night. Others, such as Lotte Fürstenberg-Cassirer (1879–1969), also continued the tradition on a smaller, but no less sophisticated scale.[35] Elsa Glaser, as the hostess of the Monday soirées, positioned herself confidently in the company of these women.

The Monday receptions themselves were relatively modest, especially when compared to similar gatherings of their time. We have no indication either that they were received as particularly avant-garde affairs, as were, for example, the evenings of the Strindberg circle in the early 1890s or the public evenings of Herwarth and Nell Walden at the Sturm Gallery in the years leading up to World War I.[36] As to the atmosphere of the Glaser evenings, Scheffler wrote: "Elsa Glaser presented herself as a spontaneous, unconventional person and could be unhinged, probing the limits of what's possible but she was enthusiastic and gifted to a rare degree. She always carried her heart on her sleeve, and she didn't mind making mistakes and admitting them like a child. Basically, she was somewhat inconvenient to all the guests, but most of them liked to be moved by her."[37]

Elsa's demise in 1932 marked the end of Glaser hospitality. This caesura seems like a mirror of its time. The National Socialist's seizure of power shortly thereafter ended the history of famous salons of the Jewish bourgeoisie, which had been at their most flourishing since the end of the nineteenth century. The emerging illiberal climate also stifled the culture of modernist conviviality, which had continued to prosper after World War I, and in whose atmosphere Expressionism, in particular, was able to thrive. Curt Glaser's dark portrait by Max Beckmann (p. 6), which found pride of place on an easel in the library, if only for a few precious years, can thus not only be read as a premonition of widowhood, but also as a late pictorial document testifying to a proud Jewish bourgeois culture in Berlin, which made itself at home in society through art.

ELSA GLASER'S LEGACY: HISTORY'S BLIND SPOTS

Until today, only one archival document of some length in Elsa's own, immediate voice has been identified (p. 27, bottom): a handwritten note she added to a letter from her husband to Karl Scheffler.[38] Yet, being portrayed by two artists such as Matisse and Munch—figureheads of European modern art—secured her place in the history books. There is no doubt that the traces of Elsa's life would be scarcer if she had been born into a family of lesser means, as the histories of art and literature have taught us. The same is true if her husband's reputation and career in the arts would not have flourished thanks to the myriad ways in which she supported him—which we read as her way of assuring her own standing. In this sense, her social position guaranteed that she would be remembered for posterity.

However, the number and variety of Elsa's portraits also indicates a personality worth painting, drawing, photographing, and writing about in letters and memoirs. Her charisma left her contemporaries little choice but to mention, document, and remember her. While these sources reveal the influence she had on her contemporaries, it remains particularly difficult to gain a better understanding of Elsa's own agency and subjectivity, as well as her intellectual position.

Thus, her intellectual prowess may in fact be more present in the historical record than previously assumed. Elsa's translation of Joachim Gasquet's book on Cézanne, first published in French in 1921, appeared in 1930 with Bruno Cassirer, who drummed up interest for the book through advertisements in *Weltkunst* and other magazines. Rosa Schapire, one of Germany's first female art-history PhDs and a collector of Expressionism in her own right, wrote in her review of the book: "The good translation and excellent production values of the book correspond to its significance."[39] Before Elsa's translation was issued in a limited edition book form, including forty-eight collotype plates of Cézanne works, two excerpts of it had been published as teasers in Cassirer's *Kunst und Künstler*, the periodical that like no other stood for a connection to the very beginnings of modernism in Berlin around 1900.[40] Besides the Gasquet translation, Elsa Glaser published at least one more translation under her name. This text, a translation of an excerpt by Christian Zervos on the art of Raoul Dufy, also appeared in *Kunst und Künstler* in early 1930.[41]

Curt Glaser became something of an "in-house writer" for Bruno Cassirer's publishing house, in particular for *Kunst und Künstler*.[42] A look at his contributions—to not only this but other periodicals—reveals a list of writings, whose scope is impressive. At the same time, besides the two translated texts by Elsa, we have no indication that she, acknowledged by most who met her to be very gifted and extraordinarily intelligent, has written a single text on her own. This is all the more curious as we have contemporaries, such as Kinoshita, who describe her in-depth engagement with art and culture.

That Curt dedicates his first book on East Asian art to Elsa is surely not only an acknowledgment of her companionship while traveling. We should consider the possibility that it functions too as a mediated mark of intellectual co-authorship. Indeed, it is not a far stretch to say that Elsa may have contributed to any number of texts attributed to Curt Glaser, not least because she would have been present for certain exhibitions or trips about which he published reports. In fact, some of the articles that were generally understood as being authored by him are signed with nothing but a "G." or "Glaser." While certainly a common practice, it ought to give us pause for thought in the case of the Glasers. Indeed, Yvonne Höfliger, relying on eye-witness testimonies, goes so far as to suggest that Elsa Glaser was considered co-author.[43]

***

Elsa Glaser was a woman that left a lasting impression on the people she met. She was an intellectual engine; an extroverted, curious person, attuned to the world and its people. As such, she deserves a rightful place in the annals of art history, and not just as "the wife of," but as one of two collaborators.

In closing, we share the words from Elsa's aforementioned note to Karl Scheffler, which capture both her indomitable spirit as well as the suffering that marked her later life (p. 27, bottom):

Dear Karlchen,

Now, I will soon be 50. Do I need to be less afraid then that you are not only secretly making fun of me. I can understand. I don't take myself too seriously either, but maybe that is not so stupid; life becomes a little easier. And that it is not always all rosy I feel is, ultimately, very cruel, only that one must not always look at it; it spoils the mood, and a jolly mood I wish you with all my heart. It hurts me to see and not be able to help when you find it difficult to always fill the half page; do not let yourself be undermined. Bloody hell.

Sincerely, also to the wife,

Elsa[44]

The authors would like to thank Allison Morehead and Peter Sproule for their insightful comments on a draft of this essay, and Judith Rauser for establishing the contact.

1 Strobl 2006, p. 17; see also the letter Curt Glaser sent to Munch on October 17, 1932, a day before the painting was being picked up by the Nationalgalerie (Munchmuseet, Oslo, MM K 2385), informing the artist about the donation.
2 Today, the painting is at the Kunsthaus Zürich. In the work's provenance, published on their website, we read: "Glaser donated *Music on Karl Johan Street* (1889) to the Nationalgalerie Berlin at the beginning of 1933 in commemoration of his first wife." collection.kunsthaus.ch/de/collection/item/5240/.
3 Strobl 2006, p. 12.
4 Cf., e.g., Höfliger 1977.
5 In this context, Sonja Niederacher speaks of "ownership structures as gender question." See Niederacher 2012, p. 9.
6 Following a visit of the Glasers in September 1930, Ernst Ludwig Kirchner wrote in a letter to Gustav Schiefler on October 16, 1930: "They were completely disturbed by the political turmoil in Germany, especially her. The formerly elegant woman has become a real Mühlendamm Jewess, deformed, vulgar, loud." See Henze 1999, p. 649. "Mühlendamm" referred to a small merchants' quarter in Berlin, and, as an expression, implied negative qualities attributed to Jewish merchants in anti-Semitic polemics. Cf. Heid/Paucker 1992, pp. 14–15.
7 Breslau address books of the 1890s and 1900s give varying descriptions of the Gebrüder Kolker business, which Hugo Kolker was running with the support of other family members.
8 Standesamt [civil registry office] Breslau, "Heiratsregister, Breslau IV, Krs. Breslau, no. 404," 1903. S Rep. 100. Landesarchiv Berlin.
9 Chichester/Sölch 2021, pp. 11–12.
10 Walravens 2012, p. 7.
11 Elsa Glaser is quoted as saying: "I cannot have any children." Given the Glasers were first cousins, it is not clear whether this refers to herself or the incapacity of the couple to produce offspring, see Kinoshita 2012, p. 81.
12 Mokutarô Kinoshita was the pseudonym of Ôta Masao, a dermatologist and writer whom the Glasers probably met through the artist Fritz Rumpf, see Kuwabara 2012, p. 69.
13 Kinoshita 2012, p. 81.
14 Ibid., p. 84.
15 Kinoshita notes in his diary that on May 21, 1911, the Glasers invited a number of artists and intellectuals, including Kinoshita, the doctor Satta Kotoji, the writer Nagata Mikihiko, and the writer and critic Seki Nyroai, into their hotel room for an evening gathering. Various outings to restaurants or the theater are undertaken in groups of multiple people, see Kuwabara 2012, p. 70.
16 Strobl 2006, S. 30–34.
17 See the essay by Judith Rauser, and the essay by Joachim Sieber in the German volume; as well as Schmidt-Burkhardt 1988. For a succinct description of the painting, see Höfliger 1977.
18 Westheim 1930. Thanks to Judith Rauser for the information.
19 No clear picture emerges as to the exact nature of the illness leading to Elsa's death, only that it must have increasingly affected her personality. While Alzheimer's disease has been suggested, Höfliger, who proposes a brain tumor as Elsa's cause of death, also speaks of an associated "geistige Umnachtung," a non-specific term to describe insanity or mental derangement, see Höfliger 1977, p. 75.
20 See the essay by Joachim Brand in the German volume.
21 Hugo Kolker, Elsa's father, died in 1915. Elsa's mother passed away in 1921. While we do not know what, if anything, Elsa inherited from her family, her inheritance would have suffered from the hyperinflation of 1921–23.
22 The work, today part of the Epstein Family Collection at the National Gallery of Art in Washington, D.C., has no known date. The Munchmuseet, Oslo which keeps an online catalog of all of Munch's work, speculatively dates it to 1913, thus positioning it among the works made during the early trips by the Glasers to Munch. However, the somber tone of the image and the fact that Elsa is holding her left hand to her ear, while her eyes stare blankly out at the viewer, suggest a symbolic hint at her increasing deafness. Curt's bald patch also indicates the passing of time.
23 Kinoshita wrote already in 1911 that he had to repeat certain things for Elsa Glaser, "as if I had a deaf companion." See Kinoshita 2012, p. 80.
24 Kuwabara 2012 p. 73.
25 Mathilde "Quappi" Beckmann to Harold Joachim, November 17, 1965, curatorial file 1964.1, The Art Institute of Chicago. Thanks to Jamie Gabbarelli for his help in obtaining the document.
26 Scheffler 1946, p. 218.
27 Scheffler 1932.
28 Höfliger, relying on eye-witness accounts, indicates that Elsa was most likely the driving force behind establishing the receptions, see Höfliger 1977, p. 72.
29 Augusta von Oertzen, "Berliner Salons: Ein Haus der Kunst," *Berliner Tageblatt*, March 31, 1929 ("Weltspiegel" supplement), p. 4.
30 For an analysis of Jewish collecting activity in Germany during this time as a strategy of bourgeois self-fashioning, see Weber 2008.
31 For a more in-depth description of the premises, see Senger 1996. The author mentions the relative smallness of the salon, where the gatherings took place, as compared to the much more spacious, elongated library of the apartment.
32 For an introduction to the circle around the Schwarzes Ferkel, see Heller 1993. Strobl also points out the affinities of Glaser with Scheffler and the generation of older critics, such as Julius Meier-Graefe, with whom the Glasers were also acquainted, see Strobl 2006, p. 151.
33 For Richter's motivations to convert in 1858, which they find in her striving for social recognition, among other things, see Uebe/Bossmann 2004, p. 134. The fact that it was also a question of social recognition can be taken from Elsa's above-mentioned conversation with Kinoshita concerning this matter.
34 Botstein 2005, p. 159.
35 Augustin 2018, pp. 354–56.
36 For a recent discussion, in particular of the gender dynamics between Herwarth and Nell Walden, see Anger 2018, pp. 31–76. For a discussion of the relationship between Herwarth Walden and Curt Glaser, cf. Strobl 2006, pp. 145–50.
37 Scheffler 1946, p. 218.
38 Among the surviving letters from Curt Glaser to Edvard Munch at the Munchmuseet in Oslo, a small number contain very short notes from Elsa, mostly sending her regards alongside her husband's signature.
39 Schapire 1930, p. 712. Another reviewer, Fritz Novotny, writes in a similar vein: "Gasquet's book, which has been available for some time in a well-translated German edition, has without exception met with an approving or even effusive reception." Novotny 1932, p. 268.
40 The two excerpts are "Aus dem Leben Cézannes," in: *Kunst und Künstler* 27, no. 7 (April 1927), pp. 286–90, and "Cézanne, Anekdoten und Aussprüche," in: *Kunst und Künstler* 28, no. 3 (December 1929), pp. 109–11. Curt Glaser had published an article in two parts on Gasquet's book in 1927 in *Kunst und Künstler*, but the excerpts in that text were translated by Margarete Mauthner, who was a regular translator for Bruno Cassirer and *Kunst und Künstler* and a prominent collector in her own right; see Glaser 1927.
41 Zervos 1930.
42 Walravens 2012, p. 12.
43 Höfliger 1977, p. 72.
44 Elsa Glaser to Karl Scheffler, n.d., [before May 1928], Akademie der Künste Berlin–Karl-Scheffler-Archiv, Scheffler 368.

Judith Rauser

THE COLLECTION OF CURT AND ELSA GLASER

"SO DISTINCTLY MULTIFACETED IS THIS, IN NO RESPECT COMMONPLACE, COLLECTION"

The "in no respect commonplace"[1] private collection of Curt and Elsa Glaser is not easy to describe or categorize for many reasons, among which the dispersal of the collection in the wake of the two auctions in May 1933 is only the most obvious.[2] In the recent research literature on Glaser, private collecting—and its relationship to the frequently emphasized interwovenness of his various spheres of activity—has played a recurring role. Some writings about Glaser have, at least cursorily, touched upon the subject with regard to individual artists and Glaser's relationship to them.[3] However, a focused investigation of the private collection of Curt and Elsa Glaser has yet to be undertaken and would certainly constitute an extensive research project. Neither the research concerning the "Glaser case" nor the current exhibition could have aimed to produce a complete scholarly reappraisal of the Glaser collection. Rather, an attempt has been made here to present its heterogeneity, as well as the gaps in the state of knowledge, from a variety of angles and in relation to previous perspectives on Glaser's life and work. Also manifest with regard to the development and shaping of the collection are the difficulties of understanding the part Elsa played in the "Glasers' success model".[4] References to the Glaser collection in the following should therefore be taken to explicitly include her person and position as well.

OUTLINE OF THE COLLECTION

Despite his enormously prolific publishing record, Curt Glaser does not appear to have considered it a priority to document his personal art holdings, for currently there is no known source that supplies anything like an inventory or a detailed account of the collection and its motivating principles. Statements in letters mostly refer to individual works, and rarely to bodies of works, to say nothing of the entire collection (with the exception of the letter to Edvard Munch on the day of the auction, in which he writes that he has freed himself from the burden of his possessions).[5] In this context, the two auction catalogs of the Internationales Kunst- und Auktions-Haus [International Art and Auction House] (pp. 14, 15) and the auction at Max Perl's (p. 32 top) come closest to providing an inventory. While they do not depict the actual genesis of the collection—what new works were added and which were let go in over two decades of collecting activity,[6] their origins, and their prices—they do provide a snapshot of nearly the entire holdings in the spring of 1933. Excluded from the roster are the paintings that Glaser held on to as long as possible, including the portrait of himself (p. 6) and the *Self-Portrait with Saxophone* (p. 87) by Max Beckmann; the paintings by Edvard Munch, Paul Kleinschmidt, and Erich Heckel that he deposited at the Kunsthaus Zürich;[7] and the art objects that would have been in the fourteen crates of Curt and Maria Glaser's household goods that were shipped to Switzerland, about which one can only speculate.[8]

To assess the question of when Curt Glaser could have made the decision to sell his collection, the approximate time that would have been needed to prepare the auction catalog had to be considered, among other factors.[9] The time window during which the preparations began was most likely between January and April 1933, but there is no way to narrow this down more precisely. In the brief time leading up to the May auctions, the process of recording and cataloguing such an extensive, heterogeneous collection would have been much more efficient if it could refer back to a previously available description. It is entirely conceivable that this was based on the expertise of the owner, since Glaser would, after all, have had an interest in adequately describing particularly the lesser-known and easily identifiable objects for inclusion in the auction. The fact that the catalog mentions details such as general condition and specific damage also speaks for the involvement of a person familiar with the collection.[10] The knowledge and information shared by Glaser would likely have been an important source, which comes to light indirectly in the ersatz "inventory" of the auction catalogs. These should therefore be regarded as meaningful documents with art-historical significance.

The catalogs provide concrete information for a quantitative classification of the auctioned works. The list of items enumerated from lot 1 to 364 under the umbrella title "Collection and Library of a Berlin Art Lover"[11] in the catalog of the International Art and Auction House contains a highly diverse assortment of objects from an upscale interior comprising numerous items of antique furniture (lot 268 to 364, including Louis XV, Louis XVI, and Biedermeier furniture), as well as numerous pieces of silver, porcelain, faience, and glass, suggesting an upper middle-class household well-equipped for large-scale entertaining. As the few surviving photographs of the interior of the apartment also show (pp. 28–29, 136), the newer reform approaches to interior design dating back to the turn of the twentieth century seem to have found no foothold in Glaser's personal environment. The historic furniture provided the setting for art objects from a wide variety of countries and epochs, which follow one another in the auction catalog without any discernible order: Chinese, Japanese, Indian, Javanese, Siamese, and Burmese pictorial works, sculptures, and objects alternate with African, Persian, Egyptian, "Hellenic", "Ancient Roman", Pompeian, and Etruscan objects, interrupted by a single modern object, the "Telefunken Radio with Loudspeaker" (lot 62). An art-historically grounded classification of these works has yet to be undertaken.

Another group of works consists of European decorative arts, sculpture, and painting of the pre-modern era, such as pieces of majolica and terracotta and over twenty wooden figures of Christ, Mary, and various apostles and saints from southern Germany dating from the sixteenth to eighteenth centuries.[12] The fact that all these objects were not organized according to geography, period, or genre, but were presented in well-considered combinations—which were only recently established in progressive exhibitions and discourses—is evident in the photograph of Glaser's study with Munch's paintings and African, Asian, and Persian sculptures on the mantelpiece and side tables (p. 29). A sketch by Beckmann (p. 86) made in conjunction with the portrait painting (p. 6) also shows Glaser sitting next to an African mask that makes eye contact in place of his downcast eyes; and between a small, presumably African, sculpture of a standing figure to his right and Munch's *Street in Kragerø*,[13] with the conspicuously branched bare tree, to the left—flanked, that is, by three representatives of his collection areas. The way the objects are presented together is reminiscent of contemporary art-historical discussions about the formal language and expression of non-European art, such as Wilhelm Worringer's *Abstraktion und Einfühlung [Abstraction and Empathy]* (1907) or Carl Einstein's *Negerplastik [Negro Sculpture]* (1915, one of the publications listed in lot 676). In a review of Einstein's text, Glaser did criticize the attempt to provide an art-theoretical systematization without an art-*historical* classification that was central for him, but also acknowledged a "path to the artistic appreciation of a subject that until now has hardly ever been viewed from anything other than a purely ethnological standpoint."[14] A less obvious but no less interesting juxtaposition is documented in the view of the library with Beckmann's portrait of Glaser (p. 28 bottom). Here, a framed relief is placed above the book- and map-laden table, with half-round edges enclosing the pictorial field of what is possibly a sketch for a ceiling decoration depicting a heavenly scene with two saints.[15] Enthroned on the table in front of this relief is a Buddha figure that picks up on the dimensions of the figures protruding from the relief's pictorial field but at the same time provides a contrast to their movement, while its hands, resting in the Buddha's lap, also establish a subtle relationship to Glaser's hierarchic appearance in the portrait. Another genre-crossing aesthetic analogy is created in the dining room by the combination of the late, expressive flower still life by Lovis Corinth[16] with two flanking and equally expressive and dynamic but Baroque figures of apostles (p. 88).[17] Such a constellation contains echoes of questions concerning the "character" of Baroque and Mannerist art and their connection to an expressive or expressionist pictorial language—an art-theoretical discussion in which Glaser's doctoral advisor Heinrich Wölfflin, as well as Wilhelm Worringer and Max J. Friedländer, had participated.[18]

Another portion of the collection documented in the auction consists of the paintings listed under numbers 226 through 267. Apart from the *Campagna Landscape*,[19] two watercolors by Corinth (lots 264–266), and the middle picture from the *Reinhardt Frieze* by Edvard Munch (lot 267), these are all Old Master works on canvas, cardboard, copper, wood, and parchment. Among these, distinct groupings can be discerned—notably, sacred art by south German and Austrian artists of the eighteenth century (including Josef Ignaz Mildorfer [1719–1775][20] and Franz Maulbertsch [1724–1796]); and Italian history painting, including two works by the circle of Tiepolo with biblical themes and a large canvas with the *Adoration of the Shepherds* by Giuseppe Maria Crespi (1665–1747; lot 251).[21] Portraits are present only in the form of a Milanese portrait of a nobleman (lot 238) and two pendants each with representations of beggars and peasants (lots 229–230; 257–258). Most extensively represented are Dutch and Flemish landscapes and history paintings from the second half of the sixteenth and the seventeenth centuries. On the one hand, this group brings to the collection the balanced painting of the Golden Age in the form of in part precious, small landscapes on wood. On the other hand, the collection also focuses on the eccentric dynamism, bright coloration, and eroticizing emphasis on corporeality in Mannerist works such as the biblical and mythological history paintings by Abraham Bloemaert (1564–1651; p. 89; lot 241) and Bartholomeus Spranger (1546–1611; lot 231)[22] as well as Joachim Wtewael (1566–1638; pp. 15, 90).[23] In their number and in part representative size, the Old Master paintings must have formed a counterpart to contemporary painting, even though the staging of the apartment as it appears in the photographs placed focus on the latter.

Little attention has also been paid thus far to the Glaser collection's enormous library, the status of which went far beyond that of a professional tool and was rather a collecting area of its own. A part of the "precious art library" was offered for sale at the International Art and Auction House under lots 482 through 699, and another part was listed a short time later under lots 1 through 325 at Max Perl's auction house.[24] Often hidden behind these numbers were wide-ranging bundles of books predominantly from the fields of European and non-European art history, philosophy, history and literature, arranged topographically, by author, epoch, and art genre and often comprising several dozen volumes. The Glasers seem to have been collectors of bibliophilic treasures as well, for the catalog of the International Art and Auction House contains not only modern editions—including many writings by art historians from the area—but also first and original editions from previous centuries and rarities such as Sebastiano Serlio's *Tutte l'Opere d'Architettura* in the 1584 edition (lot 619), Joachim Sandrart's *Teutsche Academie [German Academy]* in a splendid folio edition from 1675–80 (lot 517), or Fritz Kugler's *Geschichte Friedrichs des Grossen [The History of Frederick the Great]* with Adolph Menzel's woodcut illustrations in a first edition (lot 579), but also future classics such as the *Almanach [Almanac]* of Der Blaue Reiter (lot 647). The library thus not only reflected the collection's diverse fields of interest; it also made manifest the transitional realm between artistic production in the book arts and autonomous printmaking, which Glaser's interest encompassed in, for instance, his engagement with the woodcut.[25]

At Max Perl, in addition to books, European, Japanese, and Chinese decorative arts were on offer;[26] however, these few works were more like afterthoughts. Among the nearly one thousand lots of old and modern art, the two focal points of graphic art in the Glaser collection were distributed between some three hundred Old Master works (lots 362–689) and nearly six hundred works from the nineteenth and twentieth centuries, including Japanese woodcuts (lots 723–1333).

The fact that Glaser is considered a champion of modernism is due not only to his published writings, but also to his professional and private collecting—whereby the modern works have also received more attention, since they are typically easier to identify and present no attribution issues. Moreover, the modern portion of the collection is much more concentrated on individual artists. Here, prints predominate over individual drawings, some of which are outstanding, however. Works by Munch (lots 1081–1196) and Corinth (lots 745–839) are the most extensively represented by far. Paintings by these artists, as well as by Beckmann (lots 732–735, groups of ten to twelve prints) and Heckel (lots 877–909), were also represented in the collection even after 1933, which lends additional significance to the role of their œuvre. Among the artists the Glasers intensively collected were Ernst Ludwig Kirchner (lots 953–974), Oskar Kokoschka (lots 987–1005), Max Liebermann (lots 1020–1040),[27] Hermann Pechstein (lots 1207–1240), and Henri Matisse as the only French artist (lots 1054–1070). The stronger focus on the modern in comparison to Old Master works can be attributed not only to the emphasis on a personal connection, which is clear from the written sources, but equally to the pragmatic reasons of availability of the works on the art market.

As with contemporary art, the pattern of collecting both drawings and paintings by the same artist is present with Old Master art as well—for example in the case of Abraham Bloemaert (lots 402–407), Bartholomeus Spranger (lot 643), Roelandt Savery (1576–1639; lot 634, lot 245 International Art and Auction House), or Joachim Wtewael (lots 669 and 670). Notable highlights include the drawings of Pieter Bruegel the Elder (ca. 1526/30–1569; lots 417–419), the ink drawing with a river landscape by Claude Lorrain (1604/05–1682; lot 482), a sheet by Palma Giovane (ca. 1548–1628; lot 600), two drawings by Salvator Rosa (1615–1673; lots 26 and 27), and two from the hand of Giovanni Battista Tiepolo (1696–1770; lots 662 and 663), as well as the prints by Rembrandt (1606–1669; lots 613–619).

While the holdings of Old Master works are defined less through big names—which are not present in the collection of Dutch, Italian, and German art to the same extent as in the modern holdings—the collection can be characterized by its prevalent genres, thematic fields, and motif-related preferences. These predominate equally among the modern and contemporary works, allowing for the emergence of comparisons across epochs. The collection of fine arts thus presents itself as diverse but by no means arbitrary: mythological and biblical history, but no representations from modern history (with the exception of Menzel's illustrations); instead, there are often themes that give rise to erotic scenes; an almost neglectable number of genre representations and still lifes; hardly any portraits, apart from the ones from the hand of Matisse, Beckmann, and Munch, but instead representations of (nude) figures that were collected for reasons other than what individuals were depicted in them; and finally landscapes from all epochs. The most conspicuous gap in the collection of contemporary art in 1933 is the absence of abstract works. For instance, Wassily Kandinsky (1866–1944) was represented in the collection by a single print—significantly, a woodcut depicting a *Woman in Traditional Costume* (lot 949). Glaser's extremely critical attitude toward Kandinsky and his rejection of abstraction is reflected in his reviews, in which he disparaged the avantgardist's abstract works as, for instance, "phantoms of an idea, shells without content, framed wallpaper," and continued to condemn him into the 1930s with the scathing judgment of the decorative.[28]

A common link between Glaser's collection of old and contemporary art can be found in the concern he formulated in conjunction with the sensational "van Gogh affair" about some paintings falsely promoted as originals by the Dutchman: "We would welcome it ... if, instead of a larger purse, the deciding factor in the purchase were once again a greater understanding of art. For the true art lover chooses the piece first and only asks for the name of the artist in the second place."[29] Transposing this sentiment to the profile of the Glaser collection, aesthetic judgment is also challenged there, and in several ways. In the case of the older art, it is exercised in recognizing the quality of works that do not come with a guaranteed "artist label." With regard to contemporary art, a sure aesthetic judgment is required, since the assessment of artistic quality cannot yet rely on a canonized rating. And last but not least, the judgment necessary for collecting non-European works is founded on a much broader horizon of knowledge, which makes the collectors seem all the more fascinating.

CHANGES

A few examples will illustrate the kinds of circumstances and intentions that motivated changes within the Glaser collection. These examples relativize the notion of collecting as a continual accumulation, the way it occurs in museum practice, but also demonstrate the dynamics, freedom, and risks of private collecting, of which Glaser was certainly aware in view of his embeddedness in the complex structure of Berlin collections.[30]

His work as an art critic made him familiar with the latest developments in the art of his time, and he was accustomed to classifying these approaches as they occurred. It is therefore not surprising that Glaser acquired recent works in galleries, exhibitions, or directly from the artist. Exemplary of such acquisitions is the purchase of paintings by Henri Matisse, which found their way into Glaser's collection by way of the Galerie Bernheim-Jeune in Paris;[31] or Franz Marc's painting *The Large Blue Horses* (p. 85). Painted in 1911, the large-format work was presented at the first exhibition of the artists' group Der Blaue Reiter in 1912 and was probably acquired by Glaser at the Berlin stop of the exhibition.[32] Although this purchase looks like a coup of contemporary collecting from today's perspective, Glaser's conviction that Marc's work had artistic importance dwindled within a few years. On the occasion of the memorial exhibition in 1916 following the artist's death on the Franco-German front in World War I, Glaser posed the question: "Is Marc really among the few gifted artists who lead the way for an entire epoch through their exemplary production ...? ... The blue horses, the yellow cows, the red dogs, and whatever else the pictures of the new Marc may be called, justify every doubt."[33] With the decisive revision of his initially positive stance, Glaser sold the *Blue Horses* to the Caspari Gallery, which was founded in Munich in 1913.[34] Although the exact time of the sale cannot be established, it is unlikely that Glaser could have assessed the work in 1916 as a "decoration"[35] and a "cheerful wall ornament"[36] whose effect temporarily drowned out other works but had no duration, without having already come to the conclusion of selling it.

In other cases, a sale might be motivated not by a fundamental change in attitude toward the artist, but rather toward individual works in the Glaser collection, as is illustrated by the case of paintings by van Gogh and Matisse. For instance, the prompt sale of a van Gogh work acquired early on was caused by doubts about its authenticity—a problem that had become virulent again years later in the wake of the "van Gogh affair."[37] Glaser's appreciation of Matisse, three of whose paintings, including *Boy with Butterfly Net* (p. 83), entered the collection in 1912,[38] changed little over the years.[39] Yet he still parted with these paintings, keeping only drawings such as the striking portrait of Elsa (p. 81) and the prints. The Glasers' engagement with Matisse's work, the initial purchases, and the establishment of a personal relationship occurred during the same brief period when they had also established a connection with Munch and soon focused their attention—and their financial resources—on the latter's work. Their concern was to expand their Munch collection and strategically strengthen its quality, which explicitly involved selling or swapping pieces they owned in order to acquire works better suited to their priorities,[40] as the collector proudly reported to the artist: "The latest is that we have acquired your painting *Music on Karl Johan Street* (p. 147), which Moll owned. It is very beautiful, and we are very pleased to own it. I was able to trade it for a van Gogh, otherwise it would have been too expensive for me."[41]

In addition to interests intrinsic to the collection, however, there were also external material constraints resulting from the uncertain economic conditions of the Weimar years that could trigger sales. In 1923, for example, Glaser relates to Munch that he is no longer in a position to "preserve our art holdings in their entirety," and in 1926 that he has "also lost my freedom of movement due to the loss of my fortune."[42] Presumably, these circumstances also motivated the sale in the following year of thirteen Munch sheets from the private collection to the Kupferstichkabinett

Berlin, whose holdings Glaser had helped shape by always carefully considering which work should find a place in the museum and which in his collection, or, in the case of prints, in both places with one print each. Although there was never a consistent collector's mark or note of ownership used in the private collection, six of these prints, among them *On the Bridge* (p. 64), evince their provenance by the designation "Gl" or "Glaser" in his own characteristic handwriting. While Glaser acquired numerous Beckmann prints in one copy each for the museum and for the private collection,[43] the Berlin Kupferstichkabinett was again the beneficiary of an addition to the collection in the form of Kirchner's *Head of a Sick Man (Self-Portrait)* (pp. 58, 63 left), auctioned in 1933, which reversed a previous division into private and museum holdings: In 1922, under Glaser's aegis, two prints from the same group of works, produced during Kirchner's stay in a sanatorium in Kreuzlingen in 1917/18, entered the Kupferstichkabinett—*Portrait of Mrs. Marie-Luise Binswanger* (p. 63 right), which is inscribed on the reverse side as "Gift to the Kupferstichkabinett Berlin"[44] and documented as a gift from the artist, and *Head of the Poet Frank I.*[45] However, the collector had acquired the self-portrait as a *Sick Man,* the most powerful work from that group, for himself—a moment in which the overlap of his interests is evident, and which makes the later gift by an unknown individual of the self-portrait from the auction to the Kupferstichkabinett appear providential. Sheets such as the *Madonna* (pp. 155, 190), which Glaser had received from Munch in 1912 "as a gift in remembrance of times gone by in Berlin"[46] on the occasion of his particularly successful exhibition review, must actually have been considered inalienable by Glaser, but nevertheless found their way into the auction. The collectors probably parted with other notable pieces before 1933: the still unidentified three drawings by Édouard Manet, which were published in a facsimile portfolio in 1922,[47] or the watercolors by Paul Cézanne, which are behind Glaser in a photograph of him (p. 28 top), as well as the paintings by Kirchner and Heckel, which are documented as loans by Glaser in exhibitions in the late 1920s.[48]

FINDING DIRECTION

As tempting as the idea might seem that understanding Curt and Elsa Glaser's private collection is a way of getting closer to the couple personally, collecting remains anchored in a historical, social, and cultural context. Particularly in the multifaceted collecting culture of the capital and in view of Glaser's vast network of curators, critics, artists, and private collectors, reciprocal influences are obvious. Despite Glaser's best connections, it was not possible for him to keep up with the largest and most important Berlin collections of modern, especially French art—like those of Carl and Felicie Bernstein, Eduard Arnhold, Rudolf Mosse, Harry Graf Kessler, or Max Liebermann (with whom Glaser shared a predilection for Honoré Daumier's prints and Japanese woodcuts)—which had already been established before Glaser began collecting and also had access to other financial resources.[49] In the extremely turbulent period of the 1910s and 1920s, the Glaser collection seems to have distinguished itself from these by a finely differentiated collection profile with a focus on graphic art and contemporary German modernism receptive to French art.

With Beckmann, Glaser once again began to promote through his writing and to collect an artist who promised to take up a position as prominent and increasingly important as Munch. The two paintings by Beckmann that found their way into the collection in 1929 and 1930 and broke a new path there—only five of his works were privately owned in Berlin at the time[50]—probably speak most strongly for the desire for representation: the *Portrait of Curt Glaser* (p. 6) seems to be the only other work commissioned after Munch's paintings of Elsa and the couple (pp. 144, 145). It is the only portrait painting of Glaser at all that attempts to capture his personality in an artistic interpretation. The drawing associated with this picture (p. 86) shows an African mask that aligns Glaser personally with Eduard von der Heydt, in whose self-dramatization the collecting of non-European objects also played a prominent role and with whom Glaser was acquainted not only as a long-time patron of the Kupferstichkabinett, but also through visits to Monte Verità.[51] The painting, on the other hand, with its concentration on the shadowed, at once enigmatic and expressive face and a single attribute, has an affinity with *Self-Portrait with Saxophone* (p. 87). As far as we know, this canvas was the last to enter the collection of Curt and Elsa Glaser through purchase before their collecting activities came to an abrupt end due to the rupture of Glaser's life by political events.

Hans Purrmann's assessment that "the Glasers ... were constantly selling their works"[52] may be a retrospective view colored by his wavering goodwill towards Glaser, but it hits the mark on an essential point: the Glaser collection was a dynamic and above all "lived" collection. It offered Curt and Elsa, their friends, and like-minded acquaintances an inexhaustible object of conversation and discussion. It meant constant engagement and entailed the effort of shaping it, which ensured it against any danger of being "commonplace." The profile of the collection, like Glaser's profile as a scholar, was characterized by a kind of multiple strategy of being at the same time - and not successively—a champion of modernism, yet not simply a partisan of this faction. Old Master, contemporary, and non-European arts constituted a productive complement. Thus, all the specific objects around Glaser reflected his anchoring in scholarly debate as well as his *longue durée* perspective, which attempts to discern what is mutually illuminating and enduring both in the old and the contemporary.

1 P. Wescher (?), *Pantheon* 6, no. 3 (1933), p. XXII, quoted in Entscheid Basel 2018, p. 45.
2 See the essay by Anita Haldemann and Noemi Scherrer, p. 7.
3 Schmidt-Burkhardt 1988; Ausst.-Kat. Berlin 2003, pp. 10–11; Strobl 2006, pp. 22–26; Strobl 2012; Brand/Schulze Altcappenberg 2014, pp. 370–75; Entscheid Basel 2018, pp. 113–25; as well as the essay by Jennifer Tonkovich.
4 See the essay by Lynn Rother and Max Koss.
5 Curt Glaser to Edvard Munch, May 19, 1933, Munchmuseet, Oslo, MM K 2387.
6 On the beginnings of the Glasers' collecting activity, see the essay by Anita Haldemann and Noemi Scherrer, p. 5; Schmidt-Burkhardt 1988, p. 63; Ausst.-Kat. Berlin 2003, p. 10; Strobl 2006, pp. 22–23; Brand/Schulze Altcappenberg 2014, p. 370.
7 See the essay by Joachim Sieber in the German volume, pp. 138–39; Erich Heckel, *Badende [Bathers]*, 1911, oil on canvas, 101×125 cm, Staatliche Kunsthalle Karlsruhe, inv. 2306; Paul Kleinschmidt, *Bar*, 1931, oil on canvas, present location unknown; on Kleinschmidt, see Strobl 2006, pp. 24–25.
8 A few drawings that came with Glaser to New York and are today in the collections of the Morgan Library & Museum as well as the Art Institute of Chicago appear to have been part of the fourteen crates of household goods shipped to Switzerland. See the essays by Anita Haldemann and Noemi Scherrer, p. 8, as well as Jennifer Tonkovich, p. 32.
9 Entscheid Basel 2018, pp. 78–85.
10 Ibid., p. 79.
11 Aukt.-Kat. Berlin 1933a. The objects from this auction will be referred to in the subsequent text by their lot numbers.
12 An exception is lot 144, a Spanish figure of Christ crowned with thorns from the sixteenth century.
13 Edvard Munch, *Street in Kragerø*, 1912, oil on canvas, 96.5×122 cm, private collection, South America.
14 Glaser 1915/16, p. 141.
15 This was possibly lot 216, "Zwei Heilige und Engel, Holz, achtteilig. Süddeutsch, 18. Jahrhundert. (Auf braunem Samt appliziert)" [Two Saints and Angel, wood, eight-part, Southern German, 18th century (on brown silk)].
16 Lovis Corinth, *Blumen und Tochter Wilhelmine [Flowers and Daughter Wilhelmine]*, 1920, oil on canvas, 111×150 cm, Kunstmuseum Basel, purchased with a special loan from the Basel government in 1939. The painting was in Glaser's possession between 1929 and 1931/32. The circumstances of its sale to the Nassauisches Landesmuseum are not known. It was confiscated from that collection in 1937 as "degenerate" and wound up at the Kunstmuseum Basel in 1939 by way of the auction *Gemälde und Plastiken moderner Meister aus deutschen Museen [Paintings and Sculptures by Modern Masters from German Museums]* at the Galerie Fischer in Lucerne.
17 Estimating in relation to the height of the canvas of 111 cm, the two sculptures are probably lots 177 and 178—"Ein Paar Barock-Holzskulpturen: Apostel, Linde, mit alter Polychromie. Süddeutsch, 18. Jahrh. 140 cm hoch" [A pair of Baroque wooden sculptures: Apostles, linden wood, with old polychrome. Southern German, 18th century, height: 140 cm].
18 Engel 2018.
19 Curt Glaser inherited the *Campagna Landscape* from the estate of his brother, who died in 1931. See Dorrmann 2008, p. 57.
20 Joseph Ignaz Mildorfer, *Abschied der Apostel Petrus und Paulus [Parting of Apostles Peter and Paul]*, ca. 1760, oil on canvas, 54.8×35.3 cm, Germanisches Nationalmuseum, Nuremberg, GM 1294; other works from the Glaser collection in the Germanisches Nationalmuseum, which compensated Glaser's heirs for keeping the works in the museum, include: Joseph Heintz the Elder (copy after), *Diana und Aktäon [Diana and Actaeon]*, tempera on parchment, 10.5×16.5 cm, Germanisches Nationalmuseum, Nuremberg, GM 1296; Friedrich Brentel the Elder, *Landschaft mit Galathea, Acis und Polyphem [Landscape with Galatea, Acis, and Polyphemus]*, 1631–51, watercolor, 10.6×16.5 cm, Germanisches Nationalmuseum, GM 1295.
21 Giuseppe Maria Crespi, *Anbetung der Hirten [Adoration of the Shepherds]*, ca. 1710–25, oil on canvas, 97.5×76.5 cm, Seattle Art Museum, inv. 49.130.
22 The painting was restituted to the Glaser heirs by a private owner and sold at Christie's Old Masters Evening Sale auction in London, December 7, 2017.
23 Three other works by the artist in Glaser's possession were *Hephästus Mars und Venus überraschend [Hephaestus Surprising Mars and Venus]* (lot 244), *Urteil des Paris [The Judgment of Paris]* (lot 250), and *Taufe Christi [The Baptism of Christ]* (lot 263).
24 Aukt.-Kat. Berlin 1993a, p. 3.
25 Glaser 1920.
26 Aukt.-Kat. Berlin 1933b. Objects from this auction are referred to in the subsequent text with their lot number; see also Entscheid Basel 2018, pp. 43–50.
27 The correspondence of the Kunsthaus Zürich concerning the Liebermann exhibition there in 1923 documents a loan from Glaser: a drawing titled *Haus hinter Bäumen [House behind Trees]*; Wilhelm Wartmann to Curt Glaser, May 21, 1923, Archive ZKG/KHZ, Ausstellung, Kopienbücher der ausgehenden Post [Exhibition, copy books of outgoing mail], Archive 2001/002:023, pp. 276–79. The drawing appears in the accompanying catalog as no. 155 under the rubric "Aus verschiedenem Besitz" [from various owners] and is marked as for sale; see Ausst.-Kat. Zürich 1923, p. 13. Whether a sale took place is uncertain; in the catalog for the Max Perl auction, a charcoal drawing by Max Liebermann appears under lot 1020 that suggests a similar subject, *Landhaus im Walde [Country House in the Woods]*. It is, however, impossible to determine whether this could have been the same sheet. With thanks to Joachim Sieber for the information about the Glaser-Wartmann correspondence.
28 Glaser 1922; Glaser 1931; see Strobl 2006, pp. 196–98.
29 Glaser 1929, p. 134.
30 See the essay by Andreas Schalhorn in the German volume.
31 Perls 1962, pp. 56–59; Schmidt-Burkhardt 1988, p. 63; Strobl 2006, p. 22.
32 Hoberg/Jansen 2004, pp. 178–79, no. 159.
33 Glaser 1916, cols. 57–58.
34 Hoberg/Jansen 2004, p. 178, no. 159.
35 Glaser 1916, col. 58.
36 Ibid., col. 59.
37 Schmidt-Burkhardt 1988, pp. 66–67; Strobl 2006, p. 22.
38 Strobl 2006, p. 22.
39 Strobl 2012, pp. 236–38.
40 Strobl 2006, pp. 30–32.
41 Curt Glaser to Edvard Munch, June 13, 1916, Munchmuseet, Oslo, MM K 2309.
42 Curt Glaser to Edvard Munch, November 10, 1923, and February 23, 1926, Munchmuseet, Oslo, MM K 2346 and MM K 2354.
43 The sheets that appear both among the acquisitions of the Kupferstichkabinett Berlin between 1921 and 1924 and in Glaser's private collection that ultimately end up in the Basel holdings via the 1933 auction include: *Selbstbildnis [Self-Portrait]* (pp. 113, 133), *Grosses Selbstbildnis [Large Self-Portrait]* (p. 135), *Minette* (p. 195), *Der Zeichner in Gesellschaft [The Sketcher in Society]* (p. 134 left), *Löwenpaar [Pair of Lions]* (p. 194), *Eislauf [Ice-Skating]* (p. 194), *Sarika mit Zigarette [Sarika with Cigarette]* (p. 195), *Frau mit Halskette (Frau Parcus) [Woman with Necklace (Mrs. Parcus)]* (p. 194), *Porträt Reinhard Piper [Portrait of Reinhard Piper]* (p. 195), *Tanzendes Paar [Dancing Couple]* (134 right), *Liegende Frau (Bildnis Johanna Loeb) [Recumbent Woman (Portrait of Johanna Loeb)]* (p. 194), *Sylvester [New Year's Eve]* (p. 195), *Bildnis einer Rumänin II [Portrait of a Romanian Woman II]* (p. 196).
44 Ausst.-Kat. Berlin 2004, p. 9.
45 Ernst Ludwig Kirchner, *Kopf Dichter Frank I [Head of the Poet Frank I]*, 1917, woodcut, 54.8×41 cm (sheet), 40×27.8 cm (image), Kupferstichkabinett, Staatliche Museen zu Berlin—Preussischer Kulturbesitz, inv. 79-1922.
46 Edvard Munch to Curt Glaser, 1912, Munchmuseet, Oslo, MM N 3423.
47 Manet 1922, no. II, VIII, XV.
48 Ausst.-Kat. Berlin 1928a; the following are marked as loans from Dr. Kurt [*sic*] Glaser: "22 Erich Heckel, *Am Teich [At the Lake]*, 1911"; "52 Ernst Ludwig Kirchner, *Unter Bäumen (Fehmarn) [Under the Trees (Fehmarn)]*, um 1911"; "65 Ernst Ludwig Kirchner, Frankfurt, um 1915/16."
49 Teeuwisse 1987; Pophanken/Billeter 2001; Ausst.-Kat. Berlin 2013.
50 In a preface to an exhibition catalog in which Glaser appears as the lender of a work by Hans Purrmann, Ludwig Justi regretted the small number of works by Beckmann in private collections; Ausst.-Kat. Berlin 1928b, p. 7; Bambi 2015, p. 75.
51 Tisa Francini 2013; Brand/Schulze Altcappenberg 2014, p. 372 and note 23.
52 Hans Purrmann to Alfred J. Barr, 1951, in Barbara and Eberhard Göpel, eds., *Leben und Meinungen des Malers Hans Purrmann, an Hand seiner Schriften, Erzählungen und Briefe* (Wiesbaden, 1961), p. 250, quoted in Strobl 2006, p. 22.

Anita Haldemann

OTTO FISCHER'S PURCHASE FROM THE GLASER COLLECTION FOR THE BASEL KUPFERSTICHKABINETT IN 1933

THE MAY 1933 PURCHASE

On May 18 and 19, 1933, the Öffentliche Kunstsammlung Basel (Basel's public art collection) acquired two hundred works on paper from the collection of Curt and Elsa Glaser at Max Perl's auction no. 180 in Berlin (p. 32 top, cat. 1–200).[1] Ten days prior to that, Otto Fischer (1886–1948)—who had been the conservator (equivalent to the position of director today) of the Öffentliche Kunstsammlung (p. 105) since 1928—had made inquiries about the auction with his art historian friend Ludwig Burchard (1886–1960) in Berlin: "I recently received the catalog of an auction that will take place on May 18 and 19 at Perl's. There seem to be a lot of tempting things coming under the block, especially drawings and watercolors of the 16th to 20th centuries, as well as modern prints and drawings. If you have seen or will see these things, I would appreciate your sending word if you think it is worth the trouble going to Berlin on their account; the prices will probably be cheap?"[2]

By the time he received Burchard's response dated May 14, at the latest, Fischer would know that the works on auction were from the Glaser collection. The letter contained a detailed report on selected sheets on offer, a copy of which Burchard had also sent to the wealthy Viennese art historian and collector Antoine Edward Graf von Seilern und Aspang (1901–1978): "Here are the results of my perusal of the holdings to be auctioned at Max Perl's on 5/18 (nos. 1–681) and 5/19 (nos. 690–1373) at 3:15 pm. The price estimates at the 1st Glaser sale were partially exceeded, but only for the desirable things, and otherwise proved to be accurate. It will probably be the same this time."[3] The price comparison was with auction no. 156 of May 9, 1933, at the Internationales Kunst- und Auktions-Haus [International Art and Auction House in Berlin] ("The 1st Glaser Sale"), where Glaser had already sold some of his artworks and household items.[4] Burchard, who later became known as a Rubens scholar, had worked as an unpaid assistant at the Kupferstichkabinett in Berlin in 1913 and 1914, the same time as Glaser. He seems to have been very familiar with the latter's collection and residence, as he makes several references to where certain works had hung in his apartment (pp. 28 bottom, 29).[5]

After receiving Burchard's letter, Fischer had to act quickly. On May 16, he received carte blanche from the board of trustees to bid at the auction, which was taking place just two days later: "The board of trustees concurs that the conservator should seek to make opportune purchases at the auction of drawings and prints from the Glaser collection and the auctions of Old Master prints and Daumier at Boerner's and to later submit a report on the acquisitions."[6] The minutes of the June 8 meeting document Fischer's success: "The conservator reports on the auction of the Glaser collection in Berlin. Interest and participation were brisk; the prices were not exactly rock bottom, but remained close to the estimates, which were in themselves low. The opportunity was favorable to acquire something from the excellently curated collection that seemed of particular interest to us. The conservator felt justified in doing so. He has purchased some Old Master drawings and prints, furthermore a great number of prints at low prices as well as watercolors and drawings by Corinth (2 watercolors), Guys, Kokoschka (2 early drawings), Maillol, Rodin (1 watercolor, 1 drawing), Schwind, and Wilke, as well as rare major prints by Kirchner (3), Matisse (3), and Munch (2). The sheets are inspected and find the approval of the board of trustees. The total cost of the purchases amounts to about 3,130 francs. The conservator asks to be reimbursed for the price of the major works, amounting to 2,300 francs, and would like to cover the costs of the remaining sheets, to the amount of 830 francs, out of his discretionary fund, which has a current balance of around 1,500 francs. The president and Mr. Staechelin are in favor of granting this request in view of the beautiful and favorable purchases. The board of trustees agrees."[7]

In addition, it was decided at the meeting that these and other new acquisitions by the Kupferstichkabinett should be exhibited after the summer holidays. This plan was then implemented by the adjunct and curator of the Kupferstichkabinett, Hans Koegler, in an exhibition titled *New Acquisitions of Drawings, 1927–1933*, which was on view from October 14 to November 12.[8] Between 1922 and the relocation of the Öffentliche Kunstsammlung to its new building on St. Alban-Graben in 1936, the study room of the Kupferstichkabinett was located on the first floor of the Augustinerhof, and its exhibition spaces were on the second floor (pp. 104, 106). Due to the limited availability of space, starting in 1927 spaces for displaying the painting and sculpture collections were rented from the Kunsthalle on Steinenberg.[9] This is where Fischer presented the paintings he had purchased over the previous six years.[10]

The fact that the 200 works had been acquired from the collection of Curt and Elsa Glaser is mentioned only in the two sets of minutes of the board of trustees meeting cited above. The name Glaser does not appear in connection with the exhibition or in the annual report. Apparently, no one involved found this fact important for the public, and they had no qualms about acquiring works from the dissolved collection of a colleague who had been dismissed from a post in Berlin because of his Jewish background. Even if the matter may have been raised by the board of trustees off the record, the priority appears to have been to take advantage of the opportunity to acquire works from a high-quality collection for a favorable price in order to further develop the collection of the Kupferstichkabinett, in keeping with the current strategy.

There is no doubt that Fischer was aware of Glaser's dismissal, since on May 9 the *Basler Nachrichten* had also reported that he had been relieved of his post: "Glaser has been active in German museum service for many years and took over the management of the Staatliche Kunstbibliothek [State Art Library] after the death of Peter Jessen. At the same time, he also organized the large-scale exhibitions in the atrium of the neighboring Kunstgebäudemuseum and arranged important lecture cycles in the auditorium of the library."[11] In the letter to Burchard of May 8, Fischer made reference to the fact that many people had already fled Berlin for Paris. By this he must have been referring to the political situation and the persecution of the Jews, but he downplayed it: "It would give me great pleasure to hear from you again soon about what you are up to and how you are doing. I hope you have had no cause to flee like some foolish people whom I met in Paris."[12] Like Glaser, Burchard was Protestant but of Jewish descent. He emigrated to England with his family in 1935 because of Nazi persecution and received financial support there from Antoine von Seilern.[13]

Fischer was not of Jewish origin and therefore did not experience persecution himself. Nevertheless, at his former place of employment, the Staatliche Kunstsammlungen [State Art Collections] in Stuttgart, he had experienced the growing influence of Nazi ideology first-hand when they generated fierce opposition to certain contemporary artists and their advocates. For instance, in 1924, in his position as curator, he was deemed to belong to a "degenerate society of literary and expert elites who are alienated from the people" when he exhibited four hundred paintings, sculptures, and works on paper by artists such as Max Beckman, Karl Schmidt-Rottluff, Paula Modersohn-Becker, and Oskar Schlemmer in the *Ausstellung Neuer Deutscher Kunst [Exhibition of New German Art]*.[14] While those in the art world praised the exhibition, there was vehement criticism from right-wing conservative circles. Fischer was reprimanded, and his curatorial autonomy was curtailed.[15] These circumstances may also have prompted him to accept the position in Basel in 1927.[16]

As recorded in the minutes of the board of trustees, the prices the Basel Kunstsammlung paid for the works at the Perl auction were "not exactly rock bottom but remained close to the estimates, which were in themselves low."[17] Numerous museums benefited from low prices, which had fallen in the wake of the economic crisis of 1929, as many collectors were forced to part with their works, but the extent to which increasing emigration also affected the market—for example due to the closure of art dealerships and auction houses and the dissolution of households—is a very complex subject that can only be adequately addressed by taking a differentiated approach, for instance by drawing a distinction between older and contemporary art.[18] The fact is, that prices for art at the time were generally low. On May 22, the director of the Germanisches Nationalmuseum [Germanic National Museum] in Nuremberg, Ernst Heinrich Zimmerman (1886–1971), also wrote his colleague Ludwig Baldass (1887–1963) at the Kunsthistorisches Museum [Museum of Art History] in Vienna about how pleased he was with the inexpensive acquisitions: "At the Glaser auction I bought the sketch by Müldorfer [sic] for the large painting at the Barockmuseum and some drawings and watercolors, all dirt cheap, as indeed prices are coming down nicely on the whole."[19] The minutes of meetings of the Kunstmuseum Basel's board of trustees verify how, in view of the limited funds available for acquisition and the high demands made on the development of the collection, those responsible endeavored to pay the lowest prices possible. Additional funds for ambitious acquisitions had to be skillfully amassed, such as in the case of Paul Cézanne's sketchbooks from 1934 and 1935.[20]

The price estimates in the catalog of the Glaser auction at Perl's were set rather low, in keeping with the market conditions at the time. The actual prices attained can only be deduced through handwritten notes in extant auction catalogs, since the archive of the auction house has not been preserved (p. 32 top right).[21] The two hundred works acquired by Basel were estimated in the catalog to amount to 2,555 reichsmarks but were ultimately sold for a total of 2,296, that is, ten percent less. Taking into account the entire auction of 1,333 lots, within which considerably more individual works are bundled, the discrepancy between the estimates and the ultimate hammer prices is considerably higher. As Burchard correctly predicted, special or rare sheets fetched higher prices, including the two most important pieces purchased by the Kunstmuseum at the auction—the two major works by Edvard Munch. The color lithograph *Madonna* (pp. 155, 190) sold for 155 reichsmarks, almost a third over the estimated 120, and the *Self-Portrait* (p. 153) yielded 130 reichsmarks instead of 120.

THE CONSEQUENCES OF THE SALE

Today, the works from the Glaser collection are scattered among numerous collections throughout Europe and the United States. A group of Old Master drawings that Glaser was able to take with him to New York in 1941 was bequeathed to the Pierpont Morgan Library in New York City by his widow, Maria Glaser-Ash (pp. 162–63, 171–72).[23] Nothing is known about the current location of the majority of the works. The Öffentliche Kunstsammlung Basel—today known simply as the Kunstmuseum Basel—holds the largest known body of works from the collection of Curt and Elsa Glaser, with two hundred items.[24] The museum and its board of trustees acknowledged a moral responsibility as part of a just and fair solution reached with the heirs of Curt Glaser and his second wife, Maria, on the basis of the so-called Washington Principles.[25] This solution, in the form of financial compensation and an exhibition, which includes the present catalog, is an expression of recognition of Glaser's fate as a Jewish art historian who had been persecuted by the Nazis. Restitution did not take place, as in the spring of 1933 Glaser was still relatively free to decide what he wanted to sell and at which auction house. He was able to divide the lots between two houses and received the proceeds from the auction. He also took small, but significant part of his collection (for instance, the paintings by Edvard Munch) as well as part of his household to Switzerland. Because he took action early, with great foresight and acumen, he avoided expropriation upon emigration and was able to support himself in Switzerland from his assets and the reduced pension benefits he received from the German government.

Between 2007 and 2018, several German museums as well as the Rijksmuseum Amsterdam and two private collectors came to individual agreements with the Glaser heirs for works acquired in the auctions of May 9 and May 18 and 19, 1933—including, in some cases, restitution of works, and financial compensation in others.[26] Glaser's persecution as well as the circumstances surrounding the sale of the larger part of his collection in May 1933 have thus far been assessed rather differently, including originally in Basel, when, in 2008, the governing council of the Canton of Basel-Stadt decided against the restitution of the works.[27] In the publication of its decision regarding the restitution claim by Glaser's heirs, on June 24, 2009, the British Spoliation Advisory Panel announced that the Courtauld Institute of Art in London did not have to return the eight drawings from Glaser's collection (pp. 77, 96, 173).[28] The Courtauld Institute had obtained the works in 1978 from the estate of Antoine von Seilern, who had purchased them, on Burchard's advice, at the auction in May 1933. The British decision-making body argued that Glaser had not been forced into the auction, but rather initiated it much more on personal grounds—above all due to the death of his first wife, Elsa, in 1932. Moreover, the prices attained were in line with the market at the time and were therefore deemed fair.

The Dutch Restitution Commission came to a completely different decision, recommending, in October 2010, that the Rijksmuseum in Amsterdam return the painting by Jan van de Velde II to the heirs.[29] Similarly, in 2018 the city of Bamberg and the Museen der Stadt Bamberg returned a drawing of the east choir of the cathedral to the heirs as well.[30]

In the United States, where numerous works previously owned by Glaser are in various collections, no restitutions have yet taken place or been made public. Only the Museum of Fine Arts in Boston mentions—on its homepage, in connection with a painting by Joachim Wtewael (p. 90) from the Glaser collection—that his heirs have demanded the restitution of works from the 1933 auctions, but makes no reference to any concrete claim made by the heirs. Taking up the argument of the Spoliation Advisory Panel, they reject restitution on principle.[31]

OTTO FISCHER AND CURT GLASER

Only four brief and factual letters from 1929, in the archive of the Kunstmuseum Basel, document contact between Glaser and Fischer, who belonged to the same generation of German art historians. The subject of the correspondence was a request for photographs of paintings by Konrad Witz that Glaser had apparently sent to Basel.[32] Given the many parallels in their biographies, one would have actually expected them to have carried on a much more extensive exchange. Both completed their graduate studies of art history in 1907 under Heinrich Wölfflin in Berlin and specialized in German Old Master painting. They would have at least had to have met in that context.[33] Moreover, they also shared a research interest and publication record in the still young field of the art history of East Asia, for which both undertook lengthy travels.[34] Fischer completed his post-doctoral training in 1912 at the University of Göttingen with a thesis on Chinese painting, which he later substantially revised and published in 1923.[35] In Basel, in parallel with his position at the Öffentliche Kunstsammlung, he was also an adjunct professor of East Asian art history and taught courses when his museum work allowed. In addition, he intensified his research on Chinese art after moving to Ascona in the wake of his early retirement in 1938.[36] It was here, in the small town where Glaser also lived with his second wife for much of the time between 1933 and 1941, that the two must have met (again).

Furthermore, like Glaser, Fischer also collected art privately. Thus, for instance, he owned Alexej von Jawlensky's painting *Bagatelles* (ca. 1904) and Franz Marc's *Red Bull*.[37] Fischer's collecting activity is also documented in connection with the bequest to the Museum Rietberg[36] and the Glaser auction at Perl's, as can be seen from a letter to the auctioneer: "The books and prints arrived in good condition, but a piece broke off of one of the two porcelain jars, no. 700, quite evidently already before or during packing, as the missing piece was enclosed and wrapped in paper. Please let me know how much you or your insurance company will reimburse me for the damage, which affects me personally."[39]

THE COLLECTION STRATEGY OF THE ÖFFENTLICHE KUNSTSAMMLUNG BASEL

Another commonality with Glaser was Fischer's commitment to contemporary art. As their doctoral advisor Wölfflin had recommended, they both placed great importance on engaging with artworks through personal encounters with the artists. Thus, for instance, both were in contact with Beckmann, Max Liebermann, and Ernst Ludwig Kirchner (p. 108). While Glaser promoted modernism at the Berlin Kupferstichkabinett and then at the Kunstbibliothek, Fischer was responsible for initiating the first systematic acquisition of modern art for the collections of two museums: from 1921 to 1927 as chief curator and then director of the Staatliche Kunstsammlungen in Stuttgart, and from 1927 to 1938 as head of the Öffentliche Kunstsammlung Basel.

In Stuttgart, as the chief curator of the Staatsgalerie, Fischer had built up a modernist collection with works by Beckmann, Lovis Corinth, Otto Dix, Karl Hofer, Kirchner, Paul Klee, Otto Muelller, and Emil Nolde, but he had to fight hard for it and was repeatedly constrained by the museum's board of trustees. For example, he had to reverse the purchase of a painting by Oskar Kokoschka.[40] When Fischer took office in Basel in 1927, he was known as an energetic advocate of modernism. He was selected by Fritz Hauser (1884–1941), Social Democratic member of the governing council of the Canton of Basel-Stadt, overriding all the commissions.[41] It was thanks to Fischer's expertise as an experienced museum man and his involvement in the planning of the Kunstmuseum on St. Alban-Graben that it met all the modern technical requirements when it opened its doors in 1936.

Until the late nineteenth century, the Öffentliche Kunstsammlung Basel, which since its inception had been the property of the university, was entirely dependent on generating its own funds (bequests, entrance fees, et cetera). It was not until 1899 that the board of trustees, under the leadership of Heinrich Wölfflin, submitted a proposal to receive a fixed annual sum for its operations. In 1901, the Canton of Basel-Stadt approved a regular government contribution that, among other things, included a salary for assistants. In 1917, funds were added for the appointment of a conservator (museum director), and in 1919 for the position of a curator of the Kupferstichkabinett. This marked the beginning of the professionalization of the care of the collection, especially the scholarly treatment of the works, and created the basis for further additions to the collections, which would remain heavily dependent on private philanthropy into the future.[42] Strengthening and supplementing the existing focus of the collection on the fifteenth and sixteenth centuries remained central. Efforts to build a bridge to the nineteenth century with select works from the seventeenth and eighteenth centuries were also successful. The most significant expansion occurred in the area of Swiss art of the nineteenth and early twentieth centuries, when a collection arrived with works by Giovanni Segantini, Ferdinand Hodler, Giovanni Giacometti, and Cuno Amiet.

Even prior to Fischer's arrival in Basel, two paintings by Munch had already been acquired in 1927, something referred to with justifiable pride in the annual report as a "foray into leading contemporary art."[43] In 1930 Fischer succeeded in gradually expanding the contemporary international collection with the acquisition of works by Nolde and James Ensor, and in 1931 of Klee and another Munch. This expansion may have been "hesitant," but it must also be taken into account that the money was tight and the conservative forces in Basel were strong, and, as is the case today, every purchase had to be approved by the board of trustees.[44]

Against this background, it can be said that, despite difficult circumstances, Fischer worked steadfastly and even tenaciously on the expansion of the modern collection of the twentieth century and created a foundation on which his successor, Georg Schmidt (1896–1965), could build.

KOEGLER AND FISCHER

In Hans Koegler (1874–1950), who had been curator of the Kupferstichkabinett since 1927, Fischer had a fellow champion of modern graphic art in the Öffentliche Kunstsammlung.[45] With the purchase of an extraordinary bundle of sketches by Paul Cézanne, they joined forces to set important priorities.[46] Although Koegler was a Holbein expert, he was committed to promoting contemporary art, among other things by means of exhibitions at the Augustinerhof and guided tours, which he used to generate funds for acquisitions.[47] Helpful support was also provided by the Freunde des Kupferstichkabinetts [Friends of the

Kupferstichkabinett], which were founded in 1912 and later became the Verein der Freunde des Kunstmuseums Basel [Association of Friends of the Kunstmuseum Basel].[48]

A review of the lots acquired from Glaser's collection reveals a heterogeneous assortment of works, which, however, fit perfectly into the then-current collection strategy. The largest group consists of 105 lithographs by Honoré Daumier. On May 23, 1933, just a few days after the Glaser auction in Berlin, Fischer participated in the auction of Carl O. Schniewind's New York Daumier collection at C.G. Boerner in Leipzig. He bought thirty-one lithographs.[49] This focus had been established in 1914, with the purchase of twenty-four Daumiers, and continued to be pursued. On May 8, 1933, a week before it approved the Glaser acquisition, the board of trustees had decided to buy *Le ventre législatif* (1834), a major work by the artist, from the Hamburg Book Club. The purchase was completed for the considerable price of 216 reichsmarks.[50]

The second major focus consists of modernist drawings and prints by Beckmann (21) and Corinth (18), as well as smaller selections by Heckel (5), Kirchner (3), Klee (1), Kokoschka (3), Pechstein (5), Slevogt (2), and Thoma (2). French modernism is represented as well, by Matisse (3) and Rodin (2). While the Kupferstichkabinett had already acquired works by Corinth (1914), Slevogt (1915), Kirchner (1923), and Thoma (1924) before Fischer and Koegler came on board, the acquisitions of Beckmann, Heckel, and Kokoschka began after Fischer and Koegler took up their posts, namely in 1928. The first acquisitions of Klee and Pechstein followed in 1930 and 1931. In the annual report of 1928, Fischer states that "considerable" funds were necessary to supplement the nineteenth and twentieth century collection, especially because the higher prices of paintings set substantial limitations on such an expansion of the picture gallery: "So it seems, all the more, a duty to strive, at least in the gallery, to ensure that the leading masters are increasingly better represented with important examples of their drawings, and especially their prints. An attempt has thus been made to make up for some of the omissions of the past decades."[51]

The two lithographs by Edvard Munch purchased at the Glaser auction are major works by the artist (pp. 153, 155, 190). They perfectly complemented the existing collection of twelve prints acquired since 1923 and the three paintings purchased in 1927 and 1931.[52] Another two paintings were added later. As chance would have it, *Street in Aasgaardstrand* (1901) had been in the Glaser collection from 1913 to 1923, and Glaser sold it to the Staatliche Kunsthalle in Karlsruhe (then the Badische Kunsthalle) (p. 149). In 1934, Fischer brokered the sale of the painting to Fritz (1888–1949) and Sigrid (1887–?) Schwarz von Spreckelsen in Basel. In 1979 it came to the Kunstmuseum as a gift from Sigrid Schwarz von Spreckelsen and Sigrid Katharina Schwarz.[53] When Fischer left the museum in 1938, the Munch collection of twenty prints had grown to become a focal point of the collection, which Schmidt and Koegler's successor, Walter Ueberwasser, subsequently expanded on, so that today there are fifty prints at the museum. The assemblage of works from the Glaser collection in the Kupferstichkabinett, which encompasses two hundred items, thus played a major role in enhancing the holdings of modernist art at the Kunstmuseum Basel.

1 See also the essay by Anita Haldemann and Noemi Scherrer, p. 7.
2 Otto Fischer to Ludwig Burchard, May 8, 1933, Kunstmuseum Basel, archive, F 41-1933-05-08.
3 Ludwig Burchard to Otto Fischer, May 14, 1933, Kunstmuseum Basel, archive, F 43-1933-05-14. The letter to Antoine von Seilern contains the remark: "Some of the things that I have commented on and notified you of may surprise you. But this here is a copy of my report to Otto Fischer. That explains some of it." Ludwig Burchard to Antoine von Seilern, May 16, 1933, The Courtauld Gallery Archives.
4 See the essay by Anita Haldemann and Noemi Scherrer as well as Judith Rauser, pp. 7 and 21–22.
5 For instance: "Matisse. Framed. Was hung at Glaser's in the anteroom. Good: 1056—nice 1061." Ludwig Burchard to Otto Fischer, May 14, 1933, Kunstmuseum Basel, archive, F 43-1933-05-14, see Ausst.-Kat. Berlin 1933b, nos. 1054–70. See also Entscheid Basel 2018, pp. 46–48.
6 Minutes of the meeting of the board of trustees of May 16, 1933, Kunstmuseum Basel, archive, B1/13, p. 51.
7 Minutes of the meeting of the board of trustees of June 8, 1933, Kunstmuseum Basel, archive, B1/13, p. 58.
8 Jahresbericht 1933, p. 10. Starting in 1919, there was a separate curator responsible for the Kupferstichkabinett, who reported to the conservator (i.e., the director) of the Öffentliche Kunstsammlung. See Fischer 1936, p. 95.
9 Fischer 1936, pp. 110–11; Schmidt 1992, pp. 15–16; Meier 2009, pp. 31–32.
10 [Otto Fischer,] *Neuerwerbungen der Basler Kunstsammlung*, 1933, typescript for the exhibition in the spaces of the Kunsthalle Basel (possibly a press release), Kunstmuseum Basel, archive, F 001.042.000.000—A-K.
11 "Entlassungen," *Basler Nachrichten* 89, no. 126 (1933).
12 Otto Fischer to Ludwig Burchard, May 8, 1933, Kunstmuseum Basel, archive, F41-1933-05-08.
13 Wendland 1998, vol. 1, pp. 77–79.
14 Quoted in Meier 2011, p. 155.
15 Ibid., pp. 152–56.
16 On Fischer's decision, see ibid., pp. 159–60.
17 Minutes of the meeting of the board of trustees of June 8, 1933, Kunstmuseum Basel, archive, B1/13, p. 58.
18 On the appropriateness of the purchase prices at Perl's auction no. 180, price comparisons, and the Berlin art market, see Entscheid Basel 2018, pp. 50–78.
19 The reference is to Josef Ignaz Mildorfer. See Ernst Heinrich Zimmermann to Ludwig Baldass, May 22, 1933, Germanisches Nationalmuseum, Nuremberg, archive, old registry, purchases 1933, box 125 (quoted in Gutachten Benz/Königseder 2010, p. 50).
20 Hans 2017.
21 Entscheid Basel 2018, pp. 50–54. See also transcription of Aukt.-Kat. 1933b, copy at the Kunstmuseum Basel, library; kunstmuseumbasel.ch/curtglaser.
22 Ibid., pp. 51–52.
23 See the essay by Jennifer Tonkovich, pp. 34–35.
24 See the essay by Anita Haldemann and Noemi Scherrer, p. 4.
25 See kunstmuseumbasel.ch/curtglaser as well as the essay by Felix Uhlmann.
26 See the full list with sources, Entscheid Basel 2018, pp. 138–44. On the Kupferstichkabinett Berlin see Thielecke 2014 and the essay by Andreas Schalhorn in the German volume, p. 49.
27 Entscheid Basel 2018, p. 5.
28 Report Courtauld Institute of Art, June 24, 2009; assets.publishing.service.gov.uk/government/uploads/system/uploads/attachment_data/file/248231/0757.pdf.
29 The work came to the Rijksmuseum in 1935 by way of a gift from a private collector; see Aukt.-Kat. 1933a, lot 233 as well as Entscheid Basel 2018, p. 139.
30 Press release of February 1, 2018; museum.bamberg.de/allgemeine-informationen/provenienzforschung/restitutionen/.
31 See collections.mfa.org/objects/33583/actaeon-watching-diana-and-her-nymphs-bathing?ctx=c7e83414-1019-4428-b464-6870720b07b5&idx=0. The work was acquired by the museum in 1973 from a private collection. It comes from the first auction of May 8, 1933. See Aukt.-Kat. Berlin 1933a, lot 243.
32 Otto Fischer to Curt Glaser, January 8, January 9, and January 31, 1929, and Curt Glaser to Otto Fischer, January 28, 1929, Kunstmuseum Basel, archive, F 23-1929-01-08, F 23-1929-01-29, F 23-1929-01-31, and F 23-1929-01-28.
33 Fischer 1908. See also the essay by Anita Haldemann and Noemi Scherrer, p. 5.
34 Meier 2012, pp. 156–59, and Piechorowski 1986, pp. 25–26; on the Glasers' travels to Japan, see the essay by Lynn Rother and Max Koss, p. 15; on earlier European scholarship on the art history of East Asia, see von Erdberg 1985.
35 Fischer 2010.
36 Meier 2012, pp. 181, 192–98.
37 Jawlensky 1991, no. 78, and Hoberg/Jansen 2004, no. 201.
38 Tacier-Eugster 2019, pp. 203–05.
39 Otto Fischer to Max Perl, June 7, 1933, Kunstmuseum Basel, archive, F41-1933-06-07.
40 Meier 2012, pp. 155–56.
41 Ibid., pp. 160–61. On Hauser, see Stirnimann 2021.
42 Fischer 1936, pp. 97–98.
43 Jahresbericht 1927, p. 7.
44 Geelhaar 1992, pp. 187–89, and Meier 2012, pp. 167–81.
45 Meier 2009, pp. 31–33.
46 On Cézanne, see Hans 2017.
47 Meier 2009, pp. 32–33.
48 The Freunde made their first gift of works to the Kupferstichkabinett in 1912, with two drawings by Anton Graff; see inv. 1912.289–1912.290.
49 See the inventory of the Kupferstichkabinett, inv. 1933.234–1933.264.
50 See inv. 1933.31 and the minutes of the meeting of the board of trustees of May 8, 1933, Kunstmuseum Basel, archive, B1/13, p. 39.
51 Jahresbericht 1928, p. 12.
52 Ausst.-Kat. Basel 1985.
53 Woll 2009, vol. II, no. 486. Albert Kollmann (1837–1915), who acquired it from the artist, sold it to Glaser, who in turn sold it to the Staatliche Kunsthalle in Karlsruhe in 1929; see Tessa Rosebrock, "Drei Gemälde und ihre Geschichten. Geschichte #1: Edvard Munch, Landstrasse/Strasse in Aasgaardstrand, 1901," 2021, blog contribution online at kunstmuseumbasel.ch/de/programm/blog/2020/93.

Jennifer Tonkovich

CURT AND MARIA GLASER'S CACHE OF OLD MASTER DRAWINGS—FROM BERLIN TO NEW YORK

Seventeen sheets of paper, only three of which measure any larger than this volume, were among Curt Glaser's possessions in 1933 as he left Berlin, never to return. This modest cache of studies, mostly by minor artists, were among the remainders of Glaser's flourishing professional life when he was part of a rich intellectual circle in Germany that enjoyed the pursuit of works on paper, then a quiet corner of the art market.[1] These sheets accompanied Curt and his second wife, Maria Milch, to their new home in New York, a move Glaser may not have envisioned when penning *America Builds!*, his 1932 homage to American skyscrapers.[2] This is the story of how the Morgan Library & Museum in New York became the permanent home for a group of drawings that the Glasers managed to preserve through their journey to America.

INTRODUCING MARIA MILCH

Maria Johanna Dorothea Clara Milch (1901–1981; p. 157)[3] was born into a wealthy, assimilated German-Jewish family in Berlin, the third child of Ludwig Milch (1864–1926) and Else Kantorowicz Milch (1875–1963).[4] Preceded by two sisters, Lotte (Auguste Antonia Charlotte Barkan; 1894–1968) and Ellen (Ellen Sophie Emma Fischer; 1896–1983), Maria and her siblings would welcome a brother, Ernst, in 1903 (Ernst Moritz Ludwig Milch; 1903–1986) and another sister, Gertrude (Gertrude Franziska Rosalinde Meyer; 1911–2010), eight years later. The Milch family was originally from the Prussian town of Posen (present-day Poznań, Poland). Else's family ran a prosperous spirits and liquor business, while Ludwig's family operated a fertilizer factory. Ludwig and Else Milch relocated to Berlin around 1900 when Ludwig decided not to enter the family business.[5] Despite having earned a doctorate in chemistry, Ludwig pursued his interest in machines and founded Prometheus, a machine parts factory north of Berlin. The Milch family made their home in the nearby, elegant city of Charlottenburg. Although of Jewish heritage, Else and Ludwig were not religious, and the Milch children were confirmed members of the Lutheran community. The siblings were raised with a deep appreciation for music and art. Lotte excelled at playing the piano, and Gertrude obtained her master's degree in music education; Maria developed a beautiful singing voice, although she never performed professionally due to anxiety. Their sister Ellen studied home economics, which was considered critical to managing a cultured, upper-middle-class household.

Maria Milch first encountered Curt Glaser when she was invited regularly to attend Curt and Elsa Glasers' celebrated Monday salons, which they began holding in their large apartment at Prinz-Albrecht-Strasse in 1925. She was occasionally joined by her sister Gertrude. It is not known precisely when or how they first met, or whether the Glaser and Milch families knew each other, but the young and radiant Maria quickly became part of Glaser's circle. Maria's friendship with Curt deepened in the wake of his wife Elsa's illness and death in 1932.[6] Their bond was cemented during challenging times. By May 1933, Glaser was forced to sell his collections through a series of sales at the Internationales Kunst- und Auktions-Haus and Max Perl's auction house in Berlin. On May 20, 1933, the day after the final sale concluded, Curt and Maria were married, just as Glaser's professional situation became increasingly untenable.

Maria recorded that after their wedding service they immediately drove to Switzerland via Lake Starnberg, however, it is not certain when exactly they first arrived in Switzerland (pp. 32 bottom, 156) and if they went back to Berlin that summer.[7] When they eventually settled in Ascona, they rented a house and could unpack the fourteen crates of art and furnishings they managed to take with them. While they enjoyed a comfortable life, Curt was deeply frustrated by the loss of his profession, and Maria likely grieved the life they had in Berlin. It was in Ascona on July 22, 1935 that Maria delivered their daughter, Eva Renate Gertrud (1935–1943; pp. 17, 158).

Not long after their daughter's birth, the Glasers traveled to Florence in the spring of 1936 so Curt could make progress on a book devoted to fifteenth-century Italian art.[8] But all was not right. A letter from the Florence-based artist Hans

Purrmann to the art critic Karl Scheffler, who was a close colleague of Curt's in Berlin, makes a rare reference to the Glasers' daughter. As 1936 drew to a close, Purrmann sensed the developmental challenges facing the eighteen-month-old child, hinting that the Glasers themselves must have been struggling to accept the situation: "I often see Glaser, who now wants to stay there permanently, but I am sorry that it is not quite right with the child and its health, and I believe or feel that he is not yet aware of this matter, so that there is a constricting silence about this case between us, which prevents a truly friendly relationship!" On January 10, 1937, Scheffler responded to Purrmann, "What you say about Glaser's child coincides strangely with the impression that the pictures of the little one made on us."[9] When Renate failed to reach developmental milestones, perhaps during her second year, she was probably diagnosed with trisomy 21, commonly referred to as Down Syndrome. Apparently, Renate Glaser was placed in the care of an anthroposophically run home for children with special needs in Brissago in 1938 and later in the home called the Sonnenhof in Arlesheim near Basel, where she died on February 10, 1943.[10]

The Glasers left Florence for Switzerland in 1939; Italy signed the Tripartite Pact with Germany and Japan in 1940 and thus joined the Axis alliance in World War II. By February 1941 they decided to emigrate to the United States. They would not see their daughter again.

Soon after Curt and Maria Glaser's arrival in America on May 13, 1941, Glaser prepared to look for work. The American Council for Émigrés in the Professions has a single page noting his publications and work history and records the names of professional colleagues who were familiar with his accomplishments: "He is an internationally known scholar and expert. The following scholars and museum directors in America will vouch for his scholarship,—Messrs. Bach, Kent, and Ivins of the Metropolitan Museum of New York; Mr. Fox of the Brooklyn Museum; Drs. Lehmann-Haupt and Schapiro of Columbia University; Paul Sachs of the Fogg Museum, Harvard University; Dr. Walter Cook of the College of Fine Arts, N.Y. University; Drs. Shapley and E.F. Rothschild of the University of Chicago; Dr. Valentiner of the Detroit Museum; Mr. Eugene Schoen, architect and decorator in New York. Some of these men know him intimately and will be able to speak of his personality and administrative ability."[11]

Notwithstanding his many eminent supporters, Glaser did not find a position, and his declining health soon drove the couple to relocate to Lake Placid, a village in New York State's Adirondack Mountains. Despite the hopes that the natural atmosphere would prove therapeutic, Glaser would die of tuberculosis in November 1943.

The quantity of personal belongings the Glasers brought with them on their circuitous journey is unknown. We do know, however, that Glaser retained some of his drawing collection. That Glaser sought a home for the drawings in his possession before his death is documented by an exchange with the Art Institute of Chicago. The correspondence does not survive, but references to the Chicago museum's interest in acquiring drawings from Glaser's collection date to January 1943.[12] Unfortunately, the nature of the museum's proposal remains speculative, as the correspondence files from director Daniel Catton Rich's office from 1939 until 1945 were confiscated by the federal government as part of an investigation into "un-American activities." The government never returned the confiscated material. Since Rich handled most of the museum's interactions with dealers and collectors, the missive likely was from him rather than the curator of drawings, Carl O. Schniewind. The Glasers decided not to part with the drawings at that time, and upon Curt's death, the drawings, along with his remaining possessions, passed to his wife. She would retain a small group of Curt's drawings for the rest of her life, eventually leaving them as a bequest to the Morgan Library & Museum.

After Glaser's death, Maria Glaser returned to New York City, where she would remain until 1949. She first moved into an apartment a half-block away from Central Park West at 27 West 96th Street, but eventually moved into a rent-controlled apartment in the manicured square of Gramercy Park North at 60 East 21st Street. Unit 9a, overlooking the private, gated park, was where she would remain until her death. She resumed her life with a circle of German friends and acquaintances as well as family members who had also settled in New York City. When Curt and Maria left Berlin, Maria had also left behind much of her family. Her parents and siblings eventually fled, with her sister Gertrude emigrating to Brazil, while her mother, sisters Lotte and Ellen, and brother Ernst made it to New York.[13] Having her brother living around the corner on the next block was one of the great joys of Maria Glaser's new life without Curt.

Correspondence sent by Maria Glaser to the Kunstmuseum Basel in 1949 and 1951 reveals that she spent extended periods in France after the war.[14] She traveled to the south of France, where she stayed along the Cote d'Azur north of St. Tropez in the Villa Va et Vient, Sainte-Maxime, before moving to Paris and lodging at 29, rue Cassette, in the 6th arrondissement, close to the Luxembourg Gardens. By 1952, she returned to New York, where she would spend the remainder of her life.

Among Ernst Milch's circle of friends in New York was a cousin of the Milch family who shared the same first name: Ernst (Ernest) Eduard Ash (Asdi/Asch; 1890–1980).[15] The two Ernsts worked together and were good friends, and Maria certainly would have known Ash. In fact, they may have met before she left Berlin. On August 1, 1956, a few years after her return to the city, the fifty-five-year-old

Maria Glaser married the recently widowed Ash (p. 159). Ash's branch of the family had remained in Posen (Poznań), a German city that was annexed by Poland after World War II. He was raised in Berlin, educated as a lawyer, and fled to Holland with his second wife and two daughters in 1938. Arriving in New York in 1940, Ash began anew at a Wall Street brokerage firm and became a successful investment banker. His second wife, Hildegard Simon Ash, died in July 1955.[16] Ash and Maria were both close with her brother and shared a similar background and interest in art and music.

Ernst moved into Maria's apartment on Gramercy Park, then—and still—one of the most elegant and exclusive squares in the city. On the other side of the park stands the National Arts Club, where the Ashs were members starting in 1972.[17] At their two-bedroom city apartment, Maria installed the framed drawings collected by Glaser, and she and Ernst hung the hallways with contemporary German art, postcards from artists, as well as sculpture, painting, and ceramics they had collected. Ash had lost virtually all his belongings when the ship carrying them was torpedoed in Rotterdam harbor as he was fleeing the Netherlands, so many of the works were acquired during their time in New York. According to Ernst's grandchildren, art was stacked throughout the Ashs' apartment. As the years advanced, and without offspring of her own, Maria soon began contemplating the fate of the small cache of drawings collected by Glaser before the war.

THE BEQUEST

On March 22, 1974, Maria Glaser-Ash wrote to the Morgan Library with a missive simply addressed "Gentlemen." She was preparing her will and inquired whether the Morgan would be interested in receiving as a bequest the "small collection of Italian drawings, assembled by my former husband Dr. Curt Glaser, whose writings on graphics and other art topics are probably known to you." To elicit the Morgan's attention, she recounted that "when we arrived in this country in the forties, The Art Institute of Chicago expressed an interest in acquiring these drawings." Maria Glaser-Ash extended an invitation for "somebody" from the Library to visit her apartment to see the drawings, should the Library be interested, and encouraged them to phone for an appointment. That letter, with its enclosure, was lost in the mail, and the Morgan only learned of Maria's offer when Ernst Ash followed it up with a letter referencing his wife's overture and registering his surprise at the lack of a response.

Ernst Ash's letter landed on the desk of Felice Stampfle (1912–2000), curator of drawings at the Morgan, and she made an appointment to meet his wife on October 11, 1974. After what must have been a pleasant visit to 22nd street, Stampfle replied to her: "It was a pleasure to meet you this morning and to see the many interesting works of art on your walls, especially, of course, the older drawings which were collected by your first husband, the late Dr. Curt Glaser." Stampfle had already checked the Morgan's card catalog and reported that the Library held a number of his books, including tomes on Hans Holbein the Elder, Lucas Cranach the Elder, and early German painters. Stampfle expressed the Library's interest in the collection: "As I said to you, the twenty or so sixteenth-and seventeenth-century drawings which he brought together would be a most welcome addition to the Library's collection of drawings, should you decide, as was indicated in Mr. Ash's earlier correspondence, to leave them as a bequest. Should you desire, the bequest could be made in his [Glaser's] honor and the drawings would always carry his name."[18]

Her missive did not generate a recorded response, although Maria Glaser-Ash noted the bequest in her will. After her death in August 1981, the executors of her estate, represented by her brother Ernst Milch, contacted the Morgan concerning the bequest. In September 1981, Stampfle and assistant curator Cara Dufour Denison visited the Ash apartment to collect the drawings. As Stampfle remarked to the Morgan's director, Charles Ryskamp (1928–2010), "With a few exceptions, the drawings are unattributed and will require some study. Two of the better drawings are a small Bloemaert and a red chalk Cantarini, but probably most of them will remain 'zweite garniture' [second-rate filler]."[19] This was in the years before the Morgan accepted the vast study collection of Janos Scholz, the cellist and art collector, which contained hundreds of sheets of uncertain attribution but which constitutes a major repository for studying drawing in Italy. Since the works were received as Maria's bequest, they do not bear a credit line honoring Glaser.

But how did Maria Glaser-Ash decide that the Morgan Library was the right repository for Glaser's collection? Several possibilities emerge. In 1942, the art historian Adolph Goldschmidt, who had fled to Basel, counseled Glaser on research institutions in New York where he might find sympathetic colleagues and resources for his work. "You have 4 good libraries at your disposal, the Public Library, which is rich in regard to non-art historical things, where Mr. Cüp is an assistant in the Spencer Collection, whom you can send greetings, and which includes the incunabula, woodcuts, manuscripts etc., furthermore the Pierpont Morgan Library with their wonderful manuscripts and related literature and not the least the librarian Miss Belle (da Costa) Greene." He also mentions the "valuable books" department at Columbia University, headed by a German curator Dr. Helmut Lehmann-Haupt, and the photo archive of the Frick Art Reference Library, which unfortunately were off-limits due to restrictions on Germans.[20] Perhaps Maria recalled this early advice and found the Morgan the only one of these institutions to take a lively interest in Old Master drawings.

The New York-based dealer Eugene V. Thaw (1927–2018) had become involved with the Morgan Library more substantively in the 1960s, eventually showing his collection there for the first time in 1975, at which time he made a promised gift of his entire collection, which would amount to nearly five hundred drawings by the time of his death. The dealer had acquired a drawing directly from Maria Glaser-Ash in the 1960s, a 1914 Matisse portrait of Elsa Glaser (p. 81). Thaw owned a half-share with the London dealer Thomas Grange and sold it to the Art Institute of Chicago in 1964. Could this brief, discreet relationship with one of the museum's major patrons have led Maria to turn to the Morgan as the likely repository for her first husband's collection of drawings?

Another possibility might be someone in Glaser's circle who also had close connections to the Morgan. The museum was a particularly welcoming place for German refugees during the 1930s and '40s. Many renowned art historians had come to New York and presented lectures at the Morgan. In 1937, the Morgan hosted a talk on Holbein the Younger by Paul Ganz, the former director of the Kunstmuseum Basel. This was followed by a lecture series in 1938 by Jakob Rosenberg, who had relocated from Berlin to Boston, and sessions by Walter Friedlaender and Meyer Schapiro in 1939. Hanns Swarzenski, a close friend of Glaser's during his Berlin days, also had a close connection to the Morgan. As a specialist in decorative arts and the curator of sculpture at the National Gallery of Art in Washington, D.C., Swarzenski was engaged by the Library to catalog its collection of art objects in 1947. Speculation aside, the answer might simply be that the Morgan was celebrated for its collection of Old Master drawings and was only fifteen blocks away.

After Maria Glaser-Ash's death, her brother Ernst, sisters Ellen Fischer and Gertrude Meyer, stepdaughter Ellen Ash Peters, and her stepdaughter Renate Metcalfe's daughter Renate Brenneke served as executors of her estate. Glaser's drawings were assimilated into the Morgan's drawing collection, where they were immediately shown to scholars to resolve questions of attribution and uncover the context of these modest but intriguing works.

THE DRAWINGS

Richard Day's 1984 appraisal of the Morgan drawings underscores the generally modest nature of the seventeen sheets that ultimately formed Maria's bequest to the Library.[21] While various scholars have advanced proposals over the years, few of the drawings bear attributions to known artists, and the majority of the sheets are classified broadly under northern, central European, and Italian schools. Taking a closer look at these drawings, however, provides some insight into their appeal to Glaser and helps us conjecture why some works (and a few of them now in the Morgan's collection) remained unsold in 1933 and were among Glaser's possessions when he arrived in New York.

Surprisingly little is known about when Glaser acquired the Old Master drawings in his collection. Glaser's connection to drawings likely began during his graduate studies in Munich. During his time at the Kupferstichkabinett, he would have become familiar with the museum's holdings as well as the dealers and booksellers handling drawings in Germany and abroad as he pursued acquisitions. Curt and Elsa Glaser began building their collection after their wedding, although their efforts focused more on modern and contemporary art, including painting and sculpture.[22] The modest purchases of earlier drawings might have been a deliberate effort to avoid conflict with his responsibility to the Kupferstichkabinett. Becoming director of the Kunstbibliothek (Art Library) in 1924 may have freed him to pursue drawings without that constraint and led to more acquisitions, though until we can pinpoint the source for more of his purchases, this must remain speculative. A magazine article from March 31, 1929, devoted to Curt and Elsa's salons (p. 30) mentions northern Mannerism and southern German Rococo drawings alongside those by contemporary artists and friends, including Munch, Corinth, and Kirchner.[23]

Glaser seems to have been attracted to minor figurative drawings, many of which lacked firm attributions. While he may have enjoyed the challenge they presented, cost and affordability were likely significant factors. Glaser was not a collector of masterpiece drawings and likely saw his collecting of modest sheets by Old Masters as an intellectual and social activity. Collecting drawings was a common pursuit among learned and cultured circles in Germany, and many collectors were active on a limited scale. Curators, museum directors, and professors collected alongside merchants and manufacturers, lawyers and doctors. During the 1910s and '20s, drawings in Germany were often sold by book dealers, reflecting their quieter appeal and niche market, as well as the fact that many drawings surfaced in bound volumes. Nearly all of the sheets now in the Morgan from Glaser's collection exhibit damage consistent with mounting and removal from albums or sketchbooks. Likewise, almost all of the works reveal a minor degree of damage from light exposure, suggesting a long life spent in frames on the walls. The later Maria enjoyed living with the drawings on view, as can be seen in a photograph (p. 157) that features the framed drawing attributed to Bartholomeus Spranger (1546–1611) (p. 171 right) festooned with holiday decorations in the background. That a Berlin-based intellectual and director of the Kunstbibliothek with a rambling fourteen-room apartment and weekly salons would have sought a contingent of Old Master drawings to reflect his range of interests is not surprising, although it reflects a broader model for collecting drawings than is common today.

Glaser's sources for his drawings are largely undocumented, but a few can be identified, lending a sense of when and how he built the collection. One of the most compelling sheets in the Ash bequest is the aforementioned chiaroscuro wash study of Venus and Cupid attributed to Bartholomeus Spranger (p. 171 right). It was exhibited in the summer of 1924 as part of an exhibition organized by Edmund Schilling at the Städelsches Kunstinstitut, Frankfurt, the contents of which were published in a catalog by Georg Swarzenski.[24] All of the works were borrowed from German collections, mostly privately held. Glaser was thus recognized among other major collectors of Old Master drawings by the presence of the Spranger, placing him in the company of fellow art historians and industrialists who were enamored of *Handzeichnungen*.[25] By 1931, the drawing was listed in Albrecht Niederstein's catalog of Spranger's graphic work as belonging to "Sammlung Professor Glaser, Berlin." Konrad Oberhuber fully accepted it in his 1958 thesis on the artist and reconfirmed his opinion in 1982; it was also accepted by the renowned Goltzius scholar E.K.J. Reznicek. Since then, however, several experts have expressed some reservations, including Thomas DaCosta Kaufmann and Sally Metzler.[26] Recent examination of the sheet by Morgan curator Austėja Mackelaitė and Stijn Alsteens indicates that it probably is a copy of a Spranger drawing that is now lost or whose whereabouts is unknown, or by an artist producing "Sprangeresque" figures active at around the same time.[27]

As the sheet attributed to Spranger indicates, one unifying feature of the Morgan group is the preponderance of contemporary copies after drawings or prints by other artists. While the attribution of a roundel depicting Cimon and Pero attributed to Abraham Bloemaert (1564–1651) was debated after Reznicek and others suggested it was a copy, the original emerged at an auction in Antwerp and is now in a private Belgian collection.[28] Curiously, the sheet bears a modern collector's stamp in purple ink on the verso indicating it was in the Godin-Deheselle collection, about which almost nothing is known. The stamp was first noted in 1969, and in 2011 it appeared on a group of prints in the same auction lot by Joseph Wagner after Jacopo Amigoni and Giuseppe Zocchi. But for the sheet to have been acquired before 1941 by Glaser, it must have been stamped in the early decades of the twentieth century. A landscape by Jacob van der Ulft from the same collection, now at the Nelson-Atkins Museum of Art, Kansas City, was owned by Ernst Jürgen Otto (b. 1906; Lugt 873b),[29] suggesting that the collection was available to German buyers at some point before World War II.

A second sheet depicts a warrior in classical garb (p. 171 left). Jaap Bolten questioned whether the drawing could be connected with a painted portrait of the emperor Domitian by Abraham Bloemaert for a series devoted to the first twelve Roman emperors, a collaborative project that dates to 1616–25.[30] That portrait, however, is a bust-length profile view and does not seem to be related to the Morgan sketch. Bolten notes that the format of the drawing is closer to Aegidius Sadeler's ca. 1593 suite of prints after a series of paintings of Roman emperors by Titian and Bernardino Campi. While Bolten remarked that the "handling of the pen is unusual" for the artist, the use of abbreviated strokes and a fluid wash over a substantial underdrawing in black chalk is found in Bloemaert's drawings from the 1630s.

In addition to copies, the Ash bequest contains a contingent of sheets from artists' sketchbooks or albums that have been dismantled. That they were removed from bound volumes suggests some of them may have been procured from bookdealers. Among the most distinctive sheets is a drawing of Diana accompanied by nymphs that is inscribed with the name "Simon Merkenbenk" and the date 1632 or 1652 (p. 162). Thomas DaCosta Kaufmann suggested the sheet comes from an album amicorum, since this is the only sheet associated with the artist's name. Such albums of drawings were increasingly common in the seventeenth century in the Netherlands, Germany, and central Europe, and some of them are sources for unique drawings by otherwise unknown artists.[31] A similar sheet depicts Mercury and is signed "Jorg Ramsler" and inscribed "Prague 1593".[32] This small study also appears to be from an album and is likewise the only known drawing by this artist. DaCosta Kaufmann noted that Ramsler probably was an itinerant artist from South Germany, Austria, or Bohemia who worked at the Prague court, where Mercury was a common and popular theme.[33]

A double-sided sheet with a secure attribution to the draftsman Simone Cantarini (1612–1648) was likely removed from a sketchbook before being mounted to an album leaf (p. 163).[34] The page is covered with rapid compositional sketches in feathery strokes of red chalk, depicting Venus and her nymphs disarming Cupid on the recto, and possibly Venus and Adonis on the verso. A sheet depicting the same subject as the recto, but with the composition reversed and developed in greater detail, was sold in 2014, suggesting the Morgan sheet might be an early idea for the horizontal-format composition.[35]

The Italian drawings in the bequest include study sheets with more convincing attributions, few of which have been securely connected to a known project. In 1983, Nicholas Turner confirmed the inscribed attribution to Daniele Crespi on the *Adoration of the Magi* and pointed to a related sheet depicting the *Adoration of the Shepherds* at the Nationalmuseum, Stockholm (p. 172).[36] Giulio Bora supported the attribution and noted that the design was for one of the frescoes now in ruinous condition in the arcade at the Certosa di Pavia.[37] That the Morgan sheet bears the marks of G. Locarno (fl. 1826–40; Lugt 1691) and Giuseppe Pacini (fl. 1860–80; Lugt 2011), the latter a Florentine dealer, places it in Italy in the late nineteenth century. Some of the sheets from Pacini's holdings were sold to Ferruccio Asta in Venice, who opened a gallery in Milan in 1941. Could Glaser have bought the sheet in Milan or Florence on an earlier trip, or during the roughly four years, between 1936 and 1939, that he and Maria spent in Italy before their departure for the United States in 1941?[38] Mysteries remain, and further research along with the increasing pace of collections digitization will hopefully shed some light on many of the sheets in the bequest.

The sales of Glaser's collection in 1933, where the Kunstmuseum Basel acquired their cache of drawings, are also part of the story of the Morgan group. At least six of the drawings bequeathed by Maria Ash to the Morgan were offered at sales in 1933 and 1934.[39] According to the annotated copy of the 1933 sale from the Kunstmuseum Basel's archive, the lots seem to have sold, though no buyer was named. Were they bought-in? Or perhaps sold but uncollected? Marginal annotations indicate that bidding reached only half the estimate for the two sheets attributed to Bloemaert of a half figure in classical dress and Cimon and Pero. The single figure drawing, estimated at 30, only made 15, while the sheet with Cimon and Pero was estimated at 40 and only reached 20. These sheets must have remained with Max Perl after having failed to reach their reserve. In 1934 they were offered a second time, with the lot estimates lowered.[40] The Bloemaert figure reappeared for 20, while the sheet with Cimon and Pero was given an estimate of 35. They again failed to sell and seem to have been returned to Glaser.

These unsold works were among the possessions Glaser brought with him on his journey to America and for which Maria Ash sought a home in the years preceding her death. The Morgan's cache of drawings, as modest in an art-historical sense they may be, ultimately provides a thread of continuity from the glittering days of Glaser's Berlin salons through Maria's reinvented life in New York. Their history reflects the opportunities and uncertainties of the first half of the twentieth century.

1 Glaser still owned several paintings that he left behind in Switzerland at the time of his departure for the United States in 1941. See the essay by Anita Haldemann and Noemi Scherrer as well as Joachim Sieber in the German volume, pp. 10 and 138–39.
2 Glaser 1932.
3 My deepest thanks go to Bettina Meyer Basanow, Maria Milch Glaser-Ash's niece, for generously sharing her knowledge, experience, and family history with me, as well as to Valerie Sattler for answering my many questions and generously sharing her family photo album with me. I am also grateful for the assistance of family members who shared their recollections with me, including Renate Brenneke, Jim Peters, David Peters, Julie Dreisch, and Benjamin Livant, with a special thanks due to Jim Peters for finding the snapshot of Maria and Ernst in this essay. I am indebted to Richard Brooks, who put me in touch with the Milch family descendants after I contacted him via his blog devoted to his family's history.
4 Else was the sister of Ernst Kantorowicz (1895–1963), the German-American medieval historian whose remarkable career is chronicled in Robert E. Lerner, *Ernst Kantorowicz: A Life* (Princeton: Princeton University Press, 2017).
5 The family who remained in Posen included Ernst Kantorowicz and was involved in helping Jews flee Eastern Europe during World War II.
6 According to a Milch family written history, Elsa Glaser was ill with cancer, although this cannot be confirmed. For an investigation into the complex nature of Elsa's illness, see the essay by Lynn Rother and Max Koss, p. 19, note 19. The date of the start of Milch's relationship with Glaser was provided by her niece Bettina Meyer Basanow.
7 Letters document the Glasers in Paris during June and July and in Ascona in August, as well as in Ronco sopra Ascona in November. According to Strobl it is not clear if they returned to Berlin during the summer of 1933; for the events in 1933 leading up to the auctions, see the essay by Anita Haldemann and Noemi Scherrer, pp. 6–7.
8 According to Strobl they stayed in Florence from spring 1936 to fall 1938 or even 1939, with periodic travels. There is a script for a book about Italian art of the fifteenth century, reproduced in Walravens 2012. The carbon copy of the typescript is at the Leo Baeck Institute. With thanks to Anita Haldeman for this reference.
9 See letters nos. 15 and 16 especially in Billeter/Kennedy/Matelowski 2021, pp. 77–82. Translation by the author; with thanks to Judith Rauser for this reference.
10 See the essay by Anita Haldemann and Noemi Scherrer, pp. 9–10.
11 American Council for Émigrés in the Professions Records, 1930–1974: Box 3, Folder 43. With thanks to Melissa McCullen, project archivist, M.E. Grenander Department of Special Collections & Archives, State University of New York at Albany.
12 I am grateful to Nathaniel Parks and Bart Ryckbosch of the Art Institute of Chicago for their exceptional efforts to locate this correspondence. A copy of the letter from the museum was enclosed by Maria Ash when she first contacted the Morgan in 1974, although her initial missive was lost in the mail and never received. In a copy of Maria's letter, without the enclosure, she refers to a letter from January 23, 1943, expressing the Art Institute's interest in acquiring the drawings.
13 Ernst had been apprehended and briefly detained in the Sachsenhausen concentration camp at Oranienburg in November 1938. The camp was predominantly used for German citizens before 1940. Else Milch, the strong-willed matriarch of the family, presented paperwork documenting that they were confirmed Lutherans and convinced the National Socialists to release her son. He then traveled to New York and also moved into an apartment in Gramercy Park at 122 East 22nd Street. Holocaust museum database record: ushmm.org/online/hsv/person_view.php?PersonId=8510889. Ernst Milch was identified as "Prisoner 9080, Jew."
14 See Entscheid Basel 2018, pp. 130–31.
15 Ernst Ash's mother was Anna Kantorowicz (1864–1929), who was the daughter of Wilhelm Kantorowicz (1836–1894), the brother of Maks "Max" Kantorowicz (1843–1904), whose daughter Else Kantorowicz was Maria Milch's mother.
16 Richard G. Metcalf married Ash's elder daughter, Renata Ruth (1922– before 1960). His reminiscences about Ernst Ash are available via the Leo Baeck Institute's Center for Jewish History: archive.org/stream/lotteforrofamily1385unse/lotteforrofamily1385unse_djvu.txt.
17 With thanks to Robert Yahner, Curator and Registrar, National Arts Club, New York.
18 Felice Stampfle to Maria Ash, October 11, 1974, curatorial files, The Morgan Library & Museum, New York.
19 Felice Stampfle to Charles Ryskamp, September 23, 1981, curatorial files, The Morgan Library & Museum, New York.
20 Adolph Goldschmidt to Curt Glaser, November 1, 1942, see Walravens 1990a, pp. 109–10; with thanks to Anita Haldemann.
21 For information on drawings in the bequest not discussed in this essay, see the individual records in the Morgan's online catalog at www.themorgan.org.
22 See the essay by Judith Rauser.
23 Augusta von Oertzen, "Berliner Salons: Ein Haus der Kunst," Berliner Tageblatt, March 31, 1929 ("Weltspiegel" supplement).
24 With thanks to Martin Sonnabend for confirming Glaser's ownership of the sheet in an annotated copy of the catalogue at the Städel. The archival file for the exhibition and catalog, with the names of the many anonymous lenders, could not be located, though may be found in the reorganization of the institution's archive which is currently underway.
25 The Who's Who of lenders included: Johann Friedrich Lahmann (d. 1938), Dresden; art dealer Walther Hauth (b. 1885), Frankfurt; the art historian Dr. Leo Baer (b. 1880), Bad Homburg; publisher Dr. Curt Otto (1874–1929), Leipzig; and the art historian William Reinhold Valentiner (1880–1958), Berlin. The Spranger is marked "Privatbesitz, Berlin" along with several other sheets, though this is the only sheet that was certainly owned by Glaser.
26 For the Morgan Spranger, listed with a question mark, see DaCosta Kaufmann 1985, p. 106; Metzler 2014, p. 353, under "Indeterminate works" which "come very close to Spranger's hand, but for which the attribution remains undecided."
27 The drawing was examined by Mackelaitė and Alsteens on November 24, 2021, and they classified it as "school of Spranger" rather than by Spranger himself.
28 Copy after Abraham Bloemaert, *Cimon and Pero in Prison*, pen and brown ink, black wash, over black chalk, with opaque lead white watercolor (partially oxidized), on paper, 30.3×20.1 cm, The Morgan Library & Museum, New York, inv. 1981.34. The original is in the collection of Cecile Kruyhooft, Antwerp; see Bolten 2017, fig. 157, cat. 591a/887a; Bolten 2007, no. 591 as a related work to the lost original.
29 See art.nelson-atkins.org/objects/10957/wooded-landscape-with-figures. Otto, a businessman and art collector, was a figure at the center of the art world in the postwar period. He was director of the Kunstgutlager Schloss Celle, the holding center for looted art in the British occupation zone in Berlin, from August 28, 1945 until October 1947.
30 Bolten 2007, p. 588.
31 For example, see Robinson 2015. The Abrams album discussed by Robinson contains no fewer than eight sheets that are the only works known by the artists who signed them.
32 Jorg Ramsler, *Mercury*, pen and black ink and wash, ochre wash, white opaque watercolor, over black chalk, on laid paper, 18.6×15 cm, The Morgan Library & Museum, New York, inv. 1981.41.
33 J.K. Rowlands (undated note in curatorial file) observed that a drawing by the same artist was at the British Museum. The British Museum sheet, however, is inscribed, dated 1613, and signed by a Johannes Ramsler, whose relationship to Jorg, if any, is unknown. See DaCosta Kaufmann 1985 census.
34 Simone Cantarini, *Venus and the Nymphs Disarming Cupid*, verso: *Death of Adonis (?)*, red chalk on paper, 20×28.3 cm, The Morgan Library & Museum, New York, inv. 1981.43.
35 Christie's, London, December 2, 2014, lot 19.
36 Inv. NMH 1086/1863. Dated note in curatorial file. Richard Hemphill, at some point before 1985, proposed Antonio Molinari as the author of the sheet.
37 Bora 1984, p. 165.
38 The Lugano-based collectors Rudolf and Lore Heinemann also owned ex-Pacini sheets, as did the Milanese collector Carlo Prayer (1828–1900). Janos Scholz acquired sheets from the collection in Milan in the 1950s.
39 Aukt.-Kat. Berlin 1933b, lots 403, 406, 438, 528, 594, 611; 446 may be one of the two sheets that was recalled by the executors; Aukt.-Kat. Berlin 1934. With thanks to Judith Rauser for these references.
40 Aukt.-Kat. Berlin 1934, lots 870 and 871.

Felix Uhlmann

THE CURT GLASER CASE AND THE CHALLENGE THE WASHINGTON PRINCIPLES POSE FOR SWISS MUSEUMS

I. INTRODUCTION

Curt Glaser's fate is tragic. His legal case, no less so. Because of his Jewish descent, Glaser lost his position in Berlin. He sold the extensive art collection that he had acquired along with his first wife, Elsa, née Kolker. He then emigrated, first to Switzerland and later to the United States. He was never able to regain a foothold professionally after his emigration.[1]

In May 1933, the Kunstmuseum Basel (p. 178) acquired two hundred drawings and prints from Curt Glaser's collection at a public auction in Berlin. In 2008, Glaser's heirs contacted the museum in order to discuss the circumstances under which they were acquired. Initial negotiations failed,[2] but after being contacted by representatives of the heirs a second time, the Kunstmuseum Basel and the Kunstkommission [board of trustees] re-appraised the Curt Glaser case in 2018. They came to the conclusion that Glaser was a victim of National Socialism and that his case should therefore be adjudicated under the international agreement of the Washington Principles.[3] Negotiations were then held with the heirs to find a just and fair solution, which were successfully concluded in early 2020. In lieu of restitution of the works, the heirs received financial compensation. The Kunstmuseum and the board of trustees also decided to devote an exhibition to Curt Glaser's life (the present catalog accompanies this exhibition). The decision of the board of trustees and the Kunstmuseum Basel is documented with a detailed justification that is publicly available.[4]

Questions of restitution have repeatedly precipitated vigorous debate in Switzerland. The topic is emotionally charged, as the coverage surrounding the Bührle Collection at the Kunsthaus Zürich or the Gurlitt bequest at the Kunstmuseum Bern have demonstrated.[5] This emotional debate may somewhat obscure the view of important issues that tend to be underestimated in Switzerland, perhaps due to their rather "technical" nature. It is thus essential that these matters be discussed in a nuanced manner and that answers are not sought in simplified imperatives. The present essay is intended to help fill these gaps and contribute to making the debate more objective.

II. JURISDICTION AND PROCEDURAL ISSUES

1. CULTURAL INSTITUTIONS AND POLITICS

Unlike other European countries,[6] Switzerland does not have a central body that deals with the restitution of looted art and flight assets and issues appropriate recommendations. Although the Bundesamt für Kultur [Federal Office of Culture] has established the Anlaufstelle Raubkunst [Contact Point for Looted Art], the latter has no decision-making authority and essentially plays the role of an intermediary.[7] This has to do with the federal structure of Switzerland. Cultural policy is primarily the task of the cantons.[8] The most important art collections are in the possession of cantonal or municipal institutions or private institutions that receive substantial support from cantons or cities. The cantonal and municipal museums have a distinct legal structure. They are often decentralized administrative bodies that are partly controlled, and also heavily subsidized, by cantonal and municipal institutions.[9] In the case of the Kunstmuseum Basel, there is also a special provision that—according to article 6, paragraph 1, sentence 1 of the Gesetz über die Museen des Kantons Basel-Stadt [Law Concerning the Museums of Canton Basel-Stadt] of June 16, 1999 (Museumsgesetz, SG 451.100)—it is an "agency of the cognizant department." This means that the Kunstmuseum must fundamentally be treated as a state agency.[10] At the same time, however, the Museumsgesetz guarantees state museums autonomy: "Within the framework of the statutory provisions and the corresponding implementation regulations, museums are granted autonomy in relation to content, organization, personnel, and finances" (Museumsgesetz, article 6, paragraph 1, sentence 2).[11] This provision alone already raises the question of who should be the actual point of contact for recovery claims: the museum or the canton?

The arrangement becomes even more complicated when the question of restitution and its alternatives must be considered. In the Canton of Basel-Stadt, museum collections are the property of the University of Basel, and as such inalienable (Museumsgesetz, article 5). Because restitution under the Washington Principles cannot be legally enforced, it would, in the interpretation being put forth here, constitute a divestiture.[12] According to the Museumsgesetz, an exceptional case of divestiture requires a decision by the Regierungsrat [governing council] of the Canton of Basel-Stadt upon a joint application from the directorship of the relevant museum, the relevant museum commission, and the rectorate of the University (Museumsgesetz, article 5, paragraph 2, sentence 1).[13]

The board of trustees named in the Museumsgesetz (article 5, paragraph 2) guide, advise, and support the museum directors (Museumsgesetz article 7, paragraph 1, sentence 2). They have the right to call for the election of the director (Museumsgesetz article 7, paragraph 2) and to make decisions regarding purchases, loans, and the acceptance of gifts (Museumsverordnung [Museum Provisions] article 4, paragraph 3 lit. a–c).[14]

It follows from these basic legal principles that actual restitution requires the cooperation of a total of four institutions (government council, museum commission, museum directorate, university), but who has ultimate responsibility for what in this constellation is not readily apparent. Article 5, paragraph 2, sentence 2 of the Museumsgesetz speaks of an application by the museum directorate and the museum commission, which implies that, for restitution claims, these two bodies should prepare the matter and submit the corresponding application to the Regierungsrat. While this may seem like the appropriate approach in view of their respective expert domains on the one hand, and the autonomy guaranteed by article 6, paragraph 1, sentence 2 of the Museumsgesetz on the other, it is far from self-evident from the juridical perspective.

The issue is further complicated by the realization that returning assets is not the only possible way to handle a restitution claim. The Washington Principles speak of a just and fair solution.[15] Indeed, in the Glaser case the artworks were not returned; instead, it was agreed that compensation would be paid and Curt Glaser would be honored with an exhibition.[16] Mounting an exhibition falls within the competence of the museum. Less clear is the cognizant authority with regard to payment in the context of a just and fair solution. According to article 6, paragraph 1, sentence 2 of the Museumsgesetz, state museums are in principle also financially independent, but it is obvious that they are financed to a large extent by state funds, which means that there is at least de facto a strong state influence.

The complicated question of jurisdiction may exist in this specific form only for the Canton Basel-Stadt, but in its general complexity it is not at all unusual. Cantonal and municipal museums are embedded in a complex network of relationships to politics and civil society. Some clarification would be advisable not only for Basel, and ideally, not just as a pending restitution case that must be dealt with—often accompanied by a great deal of media scrutiny.

2. NATIONAL BODY, AD HOC ARBITRATION, OR DECISION BY THE CULTURAL INSTITUTION?

As previously mentioned, Switzerland does not have a national body for the resolution of restitution cases under the Washington Principles.[17] The main thrust of the agreement, however, points in this direction: "Nations are encouraged to develop national processes to implement these principles, particularly as they relate to alternative dispute resolution mechanisms for resolving ownership issues."[18] This provision should be seen against the background that it is often difficult for claimants to obtain a just and fair resolution in accordance with the Washington Principles in the state courts. Evidentiary problems frequently arise due to events being far in the past; complex international proceedings are time-consuming and costly; and, most serious of all, legal claims going back to the Holocaust era are in most cases past the statute of limitations.[19] The implementation of the Washington Principles thus often requires the use of alternative dispute resolution[20] as an alternative to the courts.[21]

Various parliamentary motions for the creation of a central authority have been submitted in Switzerland. Initially, the Bundesrat [Federal Council] was opposed to the proposals and also rejected the idea of vesting the Anlaufstelle Raubkunst with additional powers.[22] However, it has recently signaled its openness.[23] Recently, members of the former Bergier Commission also spoke out in favor of creating a special body.[24] However, there is no solution in sight for the next few years, which means that Switzerland will not have a national body anytime in the near future. The lack of a national body means that it falls to the institutions, or the cantonal and municipal authorities behind them, to confront the question of how to deal with restitution claims. The Washington Principles in fact require the bodies that issue the decision to be "balanced": "Commissions or other bodies established to identify art that was confiscated by the Nazis and to assist in addressing ownership issues should have a balanced membership."[25]

Five bodies existing in other countries unite expertise in jurisprudence, (art) history, philosophy, and museology, as well as include representatives from the art trade and the state administration.[26] The board of trustees of the Kunstmuseum Basel, which assessed the Glaser case, brings together considerable knowledge with the Kunstmuseum—but art-historical expertise outweighs historical knowledge of World War II and Jewish history and culture.[27] An even more problematic aspect: museum commissions of the

Canton of Basel-Stadt are primarily answerable to their associated museums, which are in turn constituted as municipal departments with a certain degree of autonomy. The members of the board of trustees are appointed by the governing council and the university.[28] While a certain—at times even great—degree of proximity to administrative and executive powers is also present in foreign bodies,[29] the fact that representatives of a museum should make decisions with regard to the cases in which that same museum is involved is at odds with the Washington Principles and with general (state) procedural guarantees,[30] even given that the preamble to the Washington Principles does take into account that participating states have different legal systems and procedures.[31]

How, then, should cultural institutions deal with restitution claims procedurally under these circumstances? One possibility is to set up an ad hoc arbitration court.[32] The problem with this solution is that for a state institution such as the Kunstmuseum Basel, this procedure has no support in current law. Furthermore, an ad hoc arbitration court is at odds with the principle of legality, and in order to set one up, a corresponding legal basis would first have to be established (which is, of course, a desideratum that can be open for discussion). Institutions that are considered private from the legal perspective have more flexibility in this area, even when strong community involvement results in commitments to the state, particularly the commitment to fundamental (procedural) rights. Accordingly, compatibility with superordinate law must at least be ascertained.[33]

As experience has shown, an ad hoc arbitration court also poses the challenge that it is difficult to find persons who, on the one hand, have the necessary expertise and, on the other hand, are sufficiently independent of the parties to the restitution proceedings.[34] Here, too, the lack of a national authority makes itself felt: there is no national precedent in Switzerland for decisions by an arbitral tribunal. It is not even clear what the applicable legal basis would be.[35] This makes a decision extremely unpredictable, *nota bene* for both sides. Procedurally, moreover, various points would have to be clarified, such as whether such a decision would be binding on the parties. Of course, if an arbitral tribunal were set up, it would be conceivable to clear up all of these points; the danger, however, is that the negotiations about the basic foundations would become nearly as time-consuming as negotiating the just and fair solution itself.

Finally, we must consider whether it should not be the task of the institution itself to decide how to position itself and develop its own practice. Should museums simply delegate the issues although they themselves are committed to provenance research?[36] It might be objected that in making decisions about restitution claims, the institutions do not have the same level of autonomy as a special body constituted for the task with equal representation. Naturally, museums are not completely free in their decisions. If they are municipal agencies, as in the Canton Basel-Stadt, or otherwise bound to the polity, this means a decision cannot be made at will.[37] Rather, as a part of the cantonal administration, museums are subject to the constitutional principles as stipulated in the Bundesverfassung der Schweizerischen Eidgenossenschaft (BV) [Swiss Federal Constitution]. On the one hand, they are bound by general substantive principles such as prohibition of arbitrary action (article 9 BV), proportionality (article 5, paragraph 2 BV), duty to safeguard public interest (article 5, paragraph 2 BV), et cetera, and on the other, by formal procedural obligations, such as granting a fair hearing (article 29, paragraph 1 BV), justification of decisions, et cetera.[38] In general, administrative authorities are trusted to make a fair decision, even when they do not have the autonomy of judicial authorities. A tax administration, for instance, makes decisions regarding the tax claims of private entities without being accused of being fixated solely on maximizing cantonal revenue.[39] In that same spirit, a municipal cultural institution can certainly be trusted to make an objective decision appropriate to the case.

Admittedly, limitations remain. With (other) decisions by administrative bodies, there is normally the possibility of judicially enforceable legal protections. No similar control of decisions made by municipal cultural institutions can be guaranteed where the final decision rests on the application of the Washington Principles. For this reason, the discussions regarding the establishment of a national body remain topical even when cantonal cultural institutions can be trusted to make appropriate judgments—incidentally, not least with a view to preserving their reputations.

3. APPLICABLE PROCEDURAL LAW

The Washington Principles do not stipulate a specific procedure but rather expect that one will be created: "Nations are encouraged to develop national processes to implement these principles, particularly as they relate to alternative dispute resolution mechanisms for resolving ownership issues."[40] Neither do the basic legal principles of the Canton of Basel-Stadt contain any specific regulations. Recall that restitution claims under the Washington Principles do not constitute an actual administrative or judicial proceeding. Rather, the procedural law for these cases has had to, and continues to need to, be developed independently.[41]

From a legal perspective, there are basically two conceivable approaches. For one thing, the restitution process can be imagined similarly to a civil suit between two parties, where the claimants are the plaintiffs, so to speak, and the cultural institutions the defendants. Indeed, certain models outside of Switzerland follow this thinking.[42] Civil proceedings analogously take place before an independent body. This logic would basically apply to ad hoc arbitration as well. It would also promote a certain fairness on the part of the institution—such as access to relevant documents—as dictated by the Washington Principles in conjunction with article 2, paragraph 2 of the Schweizerisches Zivilgesetzbuch (ZGB) [Swiss Civil Code].[43]

For Switzerland at the present moment, however—in my view—a parallel to public law is more appropriate. With regard to the Canton of Basel-Stadt, it is already called for solely on the grounds that the museums are cantonal agencies and, as explained, are both substantively and procedurally bound by the principles of the Swiss Federal Constitution as well as the Cantonal Constitution. In purely practical terms, this means, for instance, that the cantonal institutions must take into consideration elements in favor of a restitution claim. Their provenance research must be directed towards the complete assessment of the facts and an evaluation that is as accurate as possible. Their position should not be simply defensive—as a defendant would typically behave in a civil proceeding—but, as far as possible, committed to the material truth.[44] This is a high standard, but in my view ultimately the only justifiable position for cultural institutions with close ties to the state.

A central pillar of a fair process is the right to be heard (article 29, paragraph 2 BV). This means that the claimants in a restitution claim are a subject, not an object, of the proceedings. They must be given their due say in the proceedings. How to grant the right to be heard meaningfully in practical terms may be imagined in various configurations.[45] Naturally, the claimants should be presented with a draft of the historical facts and given the opportunity to comment on it. This also benefits the quality of the institution's work. Of course, the claimants should also be able to comment on the consequences of the historical facts under the Washington Principles. Whether the claimants are also heard orally is not decisive from the legal perspective, but may well be advisable in the interest of holding a transparent, factual dialogue face to face.

One difficulty does remain, however, which also arose in the case of Curt Glaser. If the just and fair solution does not lie in restitution (or a complete rejection of the same), negotiations will become inevitable sooner or later. The negotiation situation differs from the described preparation of the basis of the decision. In contrast to the latter, which demands the greatest possible transparency, negotiations can only be conducted successfully with a certain degree of confidentiality.[46]

In negotiations, it is also legitimate for the cultural institution to seek to optimally realize its own interests (which is usually what the other side does as well). Moreover, it is necessary to clarify how to coordinate the negotiation situation and the position taken by the institution in the development of the basis for the decision—both in terms of timing and substance.

In the case of Curt Glaser, a long prehistory made it obvious that the Kunstmuseum Basel and the board of trustees should first clarify their position with regard to the substance. For this reason, the decision-making process preceded the negotiations. Whether this is appropriate in every case or whether both procedures might be conducted together, especially in the constellation where a cultural institution approaches possible claimants, will not be further elaborated here.[47] In any case, it seems appropriate that in the event of differences, the claimants can demand that the museum make its position clear in a decision that can (and should) be discussed in public.

III. LEGAL FRAMEWORK

1. WASHINGTON PRINCIPLES

The Swiss Confederation has adopted the Washington Principles but not ratified them as soft law. The process is intended to be implemented within the framework of national law.[48] The Confederation considers its museums to be directly bound by the Principles, while for cantonal and municipal institutions, the museums' voluntary commitment of 1998 applies.[49] As far as can be seen, there is neither a legal obligation to be found in the cantonal or municipal principles of law, nor at the federal level, although the Federal Council has in fact committed itself to implementation.[50]

Private museums are, as such, not subject to the Washington Principles—given these have not been "recast" into corresponding national law.[51] Insofar as cantons and cities subsidize private cultural institutions, they can demand that the cultural institutions comply with the Washington Principles. From the point of view of administrative law, it appears permissible to place such a constraint on accessing funding.[52] It would, of course, make sense to discuss this question when drawing up the funding agreement, and not just when a restitution claim is made. Overall, the demands placed on institutions in various cantonal and municipal regulations or subvention agreements are likely to vary greatly, and further investigation of the question is in order.

The validity of the Washington Principles is, however, largely undisputed. The membership of most museums in the International Council of Museums (ICOM) in itself makes it seem hardly consistent to not commit to the Washington Principles at the same time.[53] As far as can be seen, no museum has spoken out openly against their application—at least among the cantonal and municipal institutions. Yet the question is not obvious for state museums, since a state authority's obligation to act in a certain way does not arise from a voluntary commitment, but as any important decision must be determined by the legislature.[54] Application of the Washington Principles as customary law should probably also (still) be rejected.[55]

2. THE TEREZIN DECLARATION

The uncertainties about legal foundations continue with the Terezin Declaration.[56] Here, it is striking that although the Swiss Confederation has adopted the Declaration,[57] when it comes to answering concrete questions reference is usually made only to the Washington Principles.[58] In each case, the Federal Council has stated in passing that the Terezin Declaration "reinforces" the Washington Principles.[59] The strong link to the Washington Principles is created in the Terezin Declaration through repeated references. In their structure and formulation, however, the sources are different: While the Washington Principles are structured similar to an international treaty, with a brief preamble followed by a list of articles, the Terezin Declaration is divided into nine chapters, each introduced by running text and in part supplemented with numbered paragraphs. In contrast to the Washington Principles, the numbered paragraphs are almost all formulated as calls or appeals ("We encourage all states ..."; "We urge all stakeholders ...," and so on). In this context, it seems reasonable to take the Washington Principles as a starting point when examining cases—as is undoubtedly the (international) practice—and to understand the Terezin Declaration as a fundamentally binding interpretation of the Principles.[60] These questions are relevant, because the wording of the two foundational documents are not always identical.[61] The Washington Principles speak of art that was "confiscated" by the National Socialists. The Terezin Declaration speaks, in the section on looted art, of "Nazi-confiscated and looted art"[62] within the broader context of "wrongful property seizures, such as confiscations, forced sales, and sales under duress of property."[63]

3. THE HANDREICHUNG OF THE GERMAN FEDERAL GOVERNMENT

In order to implement the Washington Principles and the "Joint Declaration"[64] in Germany, the federal government, the states, and the central municipal authorities have published the so-called "Handreichung" [handbook].[65] This is a "non-legally-binding orientation aid."[66] The Handreichung is applied by the German Advisory Commission.[67] As far as can be ascertained, other European commissions on looted property make no reference to it. In Switzerland, the Handreichung was applied in the case of the Gurlitt collection, which was bequeathed to the Kunstmuseum Bern, on the basis of a contract between the latter and the German government.[68] The Swiss museums take no official position on the German Handreichung (nor on the Terezin Declaration).[69]
In the case of Curt Glaser, in contrast, the Kunstmuseum Basel and the board of trustees decided to apply the Terezin Declaration in full, while the German Handreichung would be used as a supplement.[70] The latter is based not only on the Washington Principles but also on German restitution practice in the time immediately following World War II. It therefore appears entirely reasonable to occasionally take the Handreichung into account in a decision in Switzerland—namely, wherever it can offer additional insight into a specific question.[71] Similarly to administrative regulations before the Swiss courts, some consideration is certainly appropriate.[72] As far as can be seen, a full adoption of the Handreichung, however, is not advocated for Switzerland.

4. SWISS CIVIL LAW

The Bundesgericht [Federal Supreme Court] has developed a long-standing practice around the question of what due diligence must be exercised regarding provenance when acquiring works of art.[73] Swiss institutions are likely to readily feel bound by this practice. From the legal standpoint, however, these provisions are often not directly applicable, since a legal claim can only be rarely asserted. In Switzerland, although the claim for restitution of property is not subject to a statute of limitations,[74] the passage of time is nonetheless legally taken into account. The return of a lost object can also be demanded of someone who acquired it in good faith (article 934, paragraph 1 ZGB), but the latter becomes the legal owner if they have had the object continually in their possession in good faith without a challenge for over five years (article 728, paragraph 1 ZGB).[75] If the object is sold again, it gives the new purchaser ownership status. This often has the consequence that the claimant must prove not only that the original purchasing institution acted in bad faith, but also that all the previous owners (with ownership of longer than five years) acted in bad faith as well.[76] Naturally, this creates an enormous burden of proof, if it is possible at all.[77]
The fact that there is no legal claim does not, however, exclude that the restitution of the cultural property in question should be examined under the Washington Principles. Although they are "non-binding" and should fundamentally be applied within the context of the legal system: "In developing a consensus on non-binding principles to assist in resolving issues relating to Nazi-confiscated art, the Conference recognizes that among participating nations there are differing legal systems and that countries act within the context of their own laws."[78] However, the Principles are also intended to prevent institutions from "hiding" behind the civil law code and pointing to the legal context as a way of avoiding seeking a just and fair solution. The legal framework for institutions to commit themselves to the Principles voluntarily is provided by the principle of good faith: Anyone who is committed to the Washington Principles will be acting inconsistently if reference to these principles is not made later. The principle of good faith applies in equal measure in public and private law (article 5, paragraph 3 BV, and article 2 ZGB).[79]
This does not mean, however, that civil law is irrelevant for the application of the Washington Principles. Legal systems always involve expressing an assessment.[80] The more

contestable the legal position of an institution is, the more likely it is that restitution will have to be considered, and vice versa.[81] Of course, the absence of a legally binding claim cannot automatically lead to the rejection of a claim. This is precisely the situation that the Washington Principles aim to avoid.

IV. METHODOLOGICAL QUESTIONS

1. THE WANDERING GAZE

It is undisputed that dealing with restitution cases requires availability of interdisciplinary knowledge. What is less studied, however, is the question of how historical, art-historical, and legal approaches in particular differ.[82]

Assessing a restitution claim presupposes knowledge of the historical facts. At the same time, the appraisal of historical facts is dependent on the understanding of what is ultimately relevant for a judgment; otherwise, the task of appraising becomes boundless. The starting point resembles the question of the chicken and the egg: on the one hand, all the legal and moral valuations should be known; and on the other, the historical facts should be available in their entirety. In practice, this will rarely be the case.

In my view, a pragmatic approach is advisable. As a rule, certain historical facts will be known at the start of a case that will make a preliminary assessment possible. To the extent that an institution can assess which issues might be relevant for the evaluation, the appraisal of the facts can proceed with an emphasis on those issues. This is what is meant by the idea of the "wandering gaze."[83] At the same time, this process still has to allow for a certain openness. The application of the Washington Principles requires the assessment of each case on an individual basis (which is also why one must be wary of too much schematization).[84] Openness to the new and unexpected must be maintained during the process of determining a position.

Lawyers and art historians proceed differently in their treatment of the facts of the case. For lawyers, it is often sufficient if a certain element of the case is considered to be undisputed by all the parties. Thus, for example, in the assertion of a restitution claim, if it is conceded that proceeds from a sale were able to be transferred abroad, this raises the question—should the institution verify this fact or can it be taken as directly reliable (since it tends to speak against restitution). Lawyers would be content to accept such conceded facts without further ado,[85] while (art) historians would be more critical and further investigate the circumstances.[86] Neither the Washington Principles nor the practice of other institutions prescribe a clear requirement in this regard. As a result, here, too, a pragmatic approach would seem advisable in the sense that a historical reappraisal of undisputed facts can certainly be less comprehensive than in areas where both sides have very different interpretations.

2. DEALING WITH GAPS

The Washington Principles mandate that gaps in provenance should not be too hastily held against the claimants: "[C]onsideration should be given to unavoidable gaps or ambiguities in the provenance in light of the passage of time and the circumstances of the Holocaust era ... ."[87] The legal solution to gaps in the facts rests on the fact that legal principles determine which party should bear the consequences of the lack of evidence—that is, whether it will be to the detriment of the claimant or to the defendant in a civil proceeding; or, in this case, to the claimants or the cultural institution. The legal principle is found in article 8 ZGB: "Where the law does not provide otherwise, the party that derives rights from an alleged fact is the one that must prove its existence."[88] Thus, according to this rule, the claimants must prove that an artwork was confiscated, that the buyer acted in bad faith, et cetera. They carry the full burden of proof.[89] This basic rule is, however, supplemented by a large number of special rules of evidence, especially by the presumption and fiction.[90] Within this framework, a reversal of the burden of proof may occur.[91] Consideration should be given to whether such a reversal in the burden of proof would be appropriate in restitution cases under the Washington Principles. Such a logic is in part followed by the German Handreichung.[92] In Switzerland, it has in part been argued that bad faith can be assumed for transactions between 1943 and the time the Federal Republic of Germany was founded. This is based on the "London Declaration" of the Allies of January 5, 1943, which was directed particularly at neutral states and according to which any trade of goods from occupied territories was potentially invalid.[93]

In my view, if questions of proof are given too much weight, there is a danger of coming to a schematic judgment. It seems more reasonable to make a decision on each gap on an individual basis as to whose advantage or disadvantage it may fall. It is also possible that gaps do not affect the claimant or the institution in a binary way, but rather feed into the search for a just and fair solution. That is, they lie in a gray area, so to speak—which can be especially relevant in case of a waiver of restitution and negotiations over a financial settlement.[94] The lack of evidence works to the advantage or detriment of both sides and in this sense is shared.[95]

On the other hand, it is advisable to apply the guidelines of the Washington Principles for dealing with gaps in general, not only to gaps in factual knowledge. Uncertainties may also arise in questions of law, such as the temporal scope of the Washington Principles. In the case of Curt Glaser, namely, the issue arose of whether Glaser had already made the decision to sell the works in question before the National Socialists seized power.[96] If the time of the decision to sell is considered relevant under the Washington Principles (which seems plausible in light of the element of forced sale), a formal perspective would have to lead to a rejection of the claim, because the temporal scope of the Washington Principles would not apply. Such a solution, however, seems schematic, and in my view the Washington Principles certainly provide for a more flexible application of the legal principles.[97]

V. CONCLUSION

Questions of the provenance and the restitution of artworks are, and will continue to be, of concern in Switzerland. There are a great many decisions to be made—from the question of jurisdiction and the correct process and the applicable legal principles to the appropriate methodology.
Schematic simplifications are not a solution. Each case must be examined individually. This does not preclude paying sufficient attention to the overarching questions sketched out here. On the contrary, Switzerland still has some catching up to do.

My appreciation is due to Moritz Hany, MLaw, for the invaluable review of the text and the careful preparation of the footnotes.

1 For the historical details, see the essay by Anita Haldemann and Noemi Scherrer in this volume, as well as Entscheid Basel 2018.
2 In early 2008, the Regierungsrat [governing council] of the Canton Basel-Stadt rejected restitution. After representatives of the heirs contacted the Anlaufstelle Raubkunst, the governing council notified them in a letter dated October 15, 2010, that it was not willing to pursue mediation through the Confederation, citing the decision of the British Spoliation Advisory Panel of 2009, in which the Panel rejected the restitution of works from the Glaser collection acquired at the same auction where the Basel Kunstmuseum had purchased its works; see the press release of the governing council Basel-Stadt, “Rückgabeforderung an das Kunstmuseum Basel nicht gerechtfertigt,” February 19, 2008 (medien.bs.ch/nm/2008-02-19-rrbs-005.html), and Entscheid Basel 2018, p. 5.
3 Drawn up as the final statement of the Washington Conference on Holocaust-Era Assets 1998: Washington Principles 1998.
4 Entscheid Basel 2018.
5 “Streit um die Stiftung Bührle: Direktor Lukas Gloor droht, die Sammlung aus dem Kunsthaus abzuziehen,” *NZZ*, November 14, 2021; “Bührle-Sammlung: Künstlerin will ihre Werke aus dem Kunsthaus abziehen,” *NZZ*, December 23, 2021; “Stadtpräsidentin kritisiert den Kunsthausdirektor,” *Tages-anzeiger*, January 8, 2022; “NS-Raubkunst: Wie das Kunstmuseum Bern mit der Gurlitt-Sammlung umgeht,” *Süddeutsche Zeitung*, December 15, 2021.
6 In the process of implementing the Washington Principles, central bodies have been established in five countries; see Campfens 2017, pp. 332–34; CIVS 2019, pp. 19–57. These include the Beratende Kommission [Advisory Commission] in Germany (beratende-kommission.de), the Commission pour l’indemnisation des victims de spoliations intervenues du fait des législations antisémites en vigueur pendant l‘Occupation (CISV) [Commission for the Compensation of Victims of Spoliation Resulting from Anti-Semitic Legislation in Force during the Occupation] in France (civs.gouv.fr), the Spoliation Advisory Panel in the United Kingdom (gov.uk/government/groups/spoliation-advisory-panel), the *Restitutiecommissie* [Restitution Commission] in the Netherlands (restitutiecommissie.nl/), and the Kunstrückgabebeirat [Art Restitution Advisory Board] in Austria (bmkoes.gv.at/Kunst-und-Kultur/restitution/kunstrueckgabebeirat.html). There are considerable differences in the respective responsibilities, tasks, and procedures of these commissions, as the specific historical context of each country must always be taken into account; see Campfens 2018, p. 206. The number of recommendations made also differs widely; while the Austrian and Dutch bodies have issued several hundred decisions, the number in Germany and the UK ranges between twenty and thirty; see Weller 2018, pp. 84–86.
7 Bandle 2018, p. 101; Weller/Dewey 2020, p. 62.
8 Entscheid Basel 2018, p. 8.
9 Uhlmann 2019, pp. 47–55. Government funding represents 55% to 80% of the total income of the major Swiss art museums—for instance, 80% for the Kunstmuseum Basel (for 2018 and 2019, however, it was 70% and 65%, respectively); 70% for the Kunstmuseum Bern and the Museum Rietberg in Zurich; 63% for the Zentrum Paul Klee in Bern; and 55% for the Kunsthaus Zürich 55%; see Kunstmuseum Basel, *Jahresbericht* [Annual Report] *2020*, p. 59; Kunstmuseum Bern, *Jahresbericht 2020*, p. 42; Museum Rietberg, *Jahresbericht 2020*, p. 11; Zentrum Paul Klee, *Jahresbericht 2020*, p. 29; Kunsthaus Zürich, *Jahresbericht 2020*, p. 90 (figures in each case are for 2020).
10 Uhlmann 2019, pp. 54–55.
11 Clarification of this autonomy is, among other things, the subject of a planned partial revision of the Museumsgesetz. In particular, in the future it will be specified that museums are subject to the basic principles of public law concerning personnel, finances, and organization; see governing council Kanton Basel-Stadt, “Ratschlag zur Teilrevision Gesetz über die Museen des Kantons Basel-Stadt (Museumsgesetz)” [Proposal for the Partial Revision of the Law Concerning Museums of Canton Basel-Stadt], June 24, 2020 (RA 20.0907.01), p. 10; see also motion no. 17.5235.01 by Claudio Miozzari and associates of June 28, 2017, and the related report of the governing council of June 24, 2020 (RA 20.0907.0); further, see the governing council’s draft of the consultation procedures (RA 19.0402.01) (grosserrat.bs.ch).
12 Entscheid Basel 2018, p. 7. On the Washington Principles, see section III.1.
13 Ibid., pp. 6–7.
14 “Verordnung zum Gesetz über die Museen des Kantons Basel-Stadt” [Provisions of the Law Concerning the Museums of Canton Basel-Stadt] of December 19, 2000 (Museumsverordnung, SG 451.110; gesetzessammlung.bs.ch/app/de/texts_of_law/451.110).
15 Art. 8, Washington Principles 1998. For more details, see Campfens 2017, pp. 317–18; Bundesamt für Kultur, “Faktoren bei gerechten und fairen Lösungen,” March 2019; for an overview of how this is put into practice in the European countries, see Ebling/Bullinger 2019, pp. 301–03.
16 Entscheid Basel 2018, p. 165.
17 Section II.1. In this, Switzerland is not alone. Only five of the forty participating countries in the Washington Conference have created a central body; see note 6. Thus international practice is moving toward fulfilling the obligations in other ways, for instance by creating networks and informational transparency; see Weller 2018, p. 85.
18 Art. 11, Washington Principles 1998.
19 Campfens 2017, pp. 334–35. In Switzerland, claims that arise from acquisition of goods in bad faith are not subject to a limitation period, but here again complex problems arise in conjunction with proving that the first owner since the loss of the work, and all the subsequent owners, acted in bad faith;

see Section III.4.; Jolles 2015, pp. 141–42.
20 This is covered extensively in Campfens 2018.
21 Campfens 2017, p. 344; Raschèr 2009, p. 77; art. 11 of the Washington Principles is intended to "breathe life" into the Declaration and serve to actually enforce the agreements, according to a member of the U.S. delegation to the Washington Conference. Stuart E. Eizenstat, *Washington Conference on Holocaust-Era Assets: Proceedings*, February 19, 1999, p. 419 (commartrecovery.org/docs/WashingtonConferenceproceedings.pdf). In other respects, however, the proceedings of the Washington Conference are not particularly helpful for the interpretation of the guidelines. The final declaration of the follow-up conference in Theresienstadt also affirms that either the state courts or "alternative processes" should implement a just and fair solution, particularly where the application of legal provisions would prevent restitution: "Governments should consider all relevant issues when applying various legal provisions that may impede the restitution of art and cultural property, in order to achieve just and fair solutions, as well as alternative dispute resolution, where appropriate under law." Terezin Declaration 2009 (n.p.).
22 Interpellation no. 13.4027 by Josiane Aubert of November 27, 2013; Fragestunde, no. 15.5110 by Maximilian Reimann of March 9, 2015 (parlament.ch).
23 A new proposal was submitted at the end of 2021 and was met with an essentially positive response from the Federal Council; see motion no. 21.4403 by Jon Pult of December 9, 2021 (parlament.ch); Catrina/Muller-Chen 2022.
24 "Hat die Stiftung Bührle gelogen? Mitglieder der Bergier-Kommission kritisieren, ihnen seien Akten vorenthalten worden," *NZZ*, November 9, 2021.
25 Art. 10, Washington Principles 1998.
26 Woodhead 2019, pp. 8–10. Such a composition is generally described as "balanced." See CIVS 2019, p. 11; Jenkins 2015, p. 22. For some, a rotating composition depending on the case at hand has been proposed, so that necessary expertise is always available; see ibid., p. 23. Lawyers are always strongly represented in the commissions and often hold a presiding position; see CIVS 2019, p. 11. The commissions should also include members from outside the administration as well as representatives from organizations of victims of the Holocaust; see Raschèr 2009, p. 77.
27 The board of trustees spans a wide range of expertise (artists and professionals from art history, law, media, and natural sciences). The commissions outside of Switzerland have at times found it important to include a member with proven expertise in the history of World War II or Jewish history and culture; see Weller 2018, p. 90; CIVS 2019, p. 53.
28 The board of trustees explicitly commented on the question of autonomy in its *Entscheid in Sachen Curt Glaser*; see Entscheid Basel 2018, p. 8.
29 Woodhead 2019, p. 8–10.
30 Art. 30 BV, art. 6 EMRK, para. 12.1 lit. d KV BS (SG 111.100). These principles apply primarily to judicial proceedings (see BSK BV–Reich art. 30 N 6–7); however, the question arises of whether a quasi-judicial procedure would not be necessary to fulfill art. 11 of the Washington Principles.
31 CIVS 2019, p. 12.
32 Entscheid Basel 2018, p. 8.
33 Uhlmann 2019, p. 54. In its dealings with third parties with regard to these matters, the Kunstmuseum Bern considers itself essentially bound by private law; see Brülhart et al., 2021, pp. 120–21, 137.
34 On the qualifications and autonomy of members of an arbitration court, see Girsberger/Voser 2016, pp. 158–61; Berger/Kellerhals 2021, pp. 288–92.
35 The board of trustees relied particularly on the Washington Principles (with the Terezin Declaration as a "proposed interpretation"), the Code of Ethics for Museums of the ICOM, and the Swiss Civil Code. The so-called Handreichung of the German Federal Government, on the other hand, was applied only selectively when it yielded "additional insight" in particular questions; see section III of this essay and Entscheid Basel 2018, pp. 150–51. In contrast to this approach, in the case of the Gurlitt collection, the Kunstmuseum Bern applied the German Handreichung directly on the basis of an agreement with the Federal Republic of Germany and the Free State of Bavaria; see the "Vereinbarung zwischen der Bundesrepublik Deutschland und dem Freistaat Bayern und der Stiftung Kunstmuseum Bern," December 24, 2014, p. 4 (see section III.1 in this essay).
36 The obligation to conduct provenance research derives from Section 2 of the ICOM Code of Ethics for Museums; see ICOM Code 2017. Most Swiss art museums, including the Kunstmuseum Basel, are members of ICOM and in accordance with Section 7 of the Declaration are committed to following the ICOM guidelines; see Mosimann 2015, pp. 107–08. A corresponding obligation also derives from the *Declaration of Swiss Museums* of 1998.; see Mosimann 2015, pp. 106–07 (the Declaration is printed in Mosimann/Raschèr/Renold 2020, p. 1317). In Canton Basel-Stadt, the stipulations for provenance research shall in the future also be anchored at the legal level; see governing council Kanton Basel-Stadt, Ratschlag [Advisory Opinion] "Teilrevision Gesetz über die Museen des Kantons Basel-Stadt (Museumsgesetz)," June 24, 2020 (RA 20.0907.01), pp. 8, 19 (grosserrat.bs.ch).
37 On state control or incorporation, see Uhlmann 2019, pp. 54–55.
38 Ibid.; Entscheid Basel 2018, p. 7.
39 Entscheid Basel 2018, p. 8. On the impartiality of administrative authorities in general, see BSK B–Waldmann art. 29 N 33–36; Belser/Waldmann 2021, pp. 331–32.
40 Art. 11, Washington Principles 1998.
41 Entscheid Basel 2018, pp. 6–10.
42 Of particular importance is the question of whether the bodies may be invoked unilaterally or only by joint request of both the claimants and the institution. Unilateral appeal is possible with commissions in the United Kingdom, the Netherlands and Austria, whereas the Beratende Kommission [Advisory Commission] in Germany can only act upon application by both parties; see Weller 2018, p. 90.
43 BSK ZGB II–Ernst/Zogg art. 934 N 17r.
44 This is the so-called Untersuchungsmaxime [investigative principle] in Swiss law, according to which the presentation of evidence in proceedings under public law is usually the responsibility of the cognizant authority, whereas civil procedural law is guided by the principle of negotiation; see Kiener/Rütsche/Kuhn 2021, pp. 26–27. For restitution proceedings, the public law character would have the consequence that the authority would, in particular, take on the task of the extensive historical research, as is for instance the case with the French CIVS; see CIVS 2019, pp. 35–36. In addition, clarification would be necessary with regard to the question of whether the cognizant authority would only act at the request of other parties or whether it would also identify looted property and initiate proceedings on its own initiative.
45 On the proceedings of the board of trustees, see Entscheid Basel 2018, pp. 7, 9–10.
46 It should be borne in mind, however, that transparency and assumption of responsibility by the institution can certainly also be considered as part of a just and fair solution under the Washington Principles. Publishing the results of negotiations meets these objectives; see Hany 2022, p. 11.
47 A proactive approach to aggrieved parties is taken by the state in Austria; see Campfens 2017. However, the conditions under which a work owned by the Austrian federal government is restituted are standardized by law and decided by the cognizant ministries in consultation with the Kunstrückgabebeirat [Art Restitution Advisory Board], Arts. 1 and 3 Kunstrückgabegesetz (KRG) BGBl I 181/1998. Negotiations are therefore likely to be limited to organizational points. There have also been cases in Switzerland where an institution proactively approached former owners; see press release by the Historisches und Völkerkundemuseum St. Gallen, "HVM übergibt den Erben einer jüdischen Kunstsammlerin zwei Silberpokale in Segelschiff-Form," November 6, 2017, hvmsg.ch/medien_presse.php.
48 See notes 18, 40.
49 Printed in Mosimann/Raschèr/Renold 2020, p. 1317. On the applicability of the Washington Principles for Swiss museums, see Mosimann 2015, pp. 105–06.
50 Art. 11, Washington Principles 1998; mention is made of the Washington Principles in art. 4, para. 1e of the Ordinance of the FDHA on the Funding Concept for the Support of Museums, Collections and Third-Party Networks for the Preservation of Cultural Heritage of November 29, 2016 (SR 442.121.1), see Catrina/Müller-Chen 2022..
51 Bandle 2018, pp. 107–08. The Federal Council has expressed its views on the question of extension to private entities in a statement in response to a motion in 2014; see Federal Council statement of August 20, 2014 on the motion "Looted Art: Strengthen the Binding Force of the Washington Guidelines Internationally," no. 14.3480 of June 18, 2014 (parlament.ch). The Federal Council was not prepared to extend applicability unilaterally but emphasized the "signal function" that the Washington Principles also had for private parties. The extension of applicability to private parties was one of the demands in the Terezin Declaration, see Terezin Declaration 2009, p. 4.
52 On ancillary clauses in ordinances, see Karlen 2018, pp. 206–07. On subsidies in the cultural section, see Uhlmann 2019, pp. 47–49. The new subsidy contract with the Kunsthaus Zürich is now public; for the city council resolution see STRB Nr. 0201/2022, online via stadt-zuerich.ch/strb.
53 See in particular Section 6.3 of the ICOM

Code of Ethics for Museums: "When a country or people of origin seeks the restitution of an object or specimen that can be demonstrated to have been exported or otherwise transferred in violation of the principles of international and national conventions ... the museum concerned should, if legally free to do so, take prompt and responsible steps to cooperate in its return." ICOM Code 2017.

54 One might think of the obligation to act in good faith; see section III.4 in this essay.

55 BSK ZGB II—Ernst/Zogg art. 934 N 17p.

56 Terezin Declaration 2009.

57 EDI/EDA, *Bericht EDI/EDA über den Stand der Arbeiten des Bundes im Bereich der NS-Raubkunst im Zeitraum von 2011–2016*, October 24, 2019, p. 1 (bak.admin.ch).

58 Entscheid Basel 2018, p. 148.

59 Fragestunde, no. 14.5664 by Alec von Graffenried, December 8, 2014; motion no. 14.3480 by Mathias Reynard, June 18, 2014 (parlament.ch).

60 This is how it is handled in the outcome of the board of trustees; see Entscheid Basel 2018, pp. 150–51. It should be noted that the Terezin Declaration also addresses issues that are not mentioned in the Washington Principles, such as the treatment of Jewish cemeteries, historical education, and the commemoration of the Holocaust. For an interpretation of the Washington Principles, the chapter on "Nazi-Confiscated and Looted Art" should in particular be consulted. On the limited impact of the Terezin Declaration on the international practice of restitution, see Demarsin 2011, pp. 144–45.

61 Entscheid Basel 2018, p. 148.

62 Terezin Declaration 2009, p. 4.

63 Ibid., p. 2.

64 *Erklärung der Bundesregierung, der Länder und der kommunalen Spitzenverbände zur Auffindung und zur Rückgabe NS-verfolgungsbedingt entzogenen Kulturgutes, insbesondere aus jüdischem Besitz*, December 9, 1999 (beratende-kommission.de).

65 *Handreichung zur Umsetzung der Erklärung der Bundesregierung, der Länder und der kommunalen Spitzenverbände zur Auffindung und zur Rückgabe NS-verfolgungsbedingt entzogenen Kulturgutes, insbesondere aus jüdischem Besitz*, December 1999 (beratende-kommission.de).

66 Ibid., p. 31.

67 *Verfahrensordnung der Beratenden Kommission im Zusammenhang mit der Rückgabe NS-verfolgungsbedingt entzogenen Kulturguts, insbesondere aus jüdischem Besitz*, November 2, 2016, art. 6, para. 3 b (beratende-kommission.de).

68 Vereinbarung 2014.

69 In the case of the Bührle Collection, the loan agreement between the Zürcher Kunstgesellschaft and the collection, which is now public, indicates that the Terezin Declaration shall apply for provenance research; see *Vereinbarung zwischen der Stiftung Sammlung E. G. Bührle und der Zürcher Kunstgesellschaft*, August 5, 2021, p. 4 (kunsthaus.ch/sammlung/private-sammlungen/emil-buehrle/). Interestingly, the loan agreement refers to the concept of "cultural property expropriated by the Nazis in the context of persecution." This language does not appear in the translation of the declaration used by the Bundesamt für Kultur but is used in Germany, e.g. in the Gemeinsame Erklärung (see note 64), the Handreichung (see note 65), and the translation of the Terezin Declaration used by German authorities (kulturgutverluste.de, heading "Theresienstaedter-Erklaerung").

70 Entscheid Basel 2018, pp. 150–51.

71 Ibid.

72 On the "external effect" of administrative regulations, see Egli 2011, pp. 1162–63.

73 This is exemplified in the judgment issued in BGE 139 III 305 (https://bger.li/139-III-305). For extensive treatment of this issue, see Mosimann 2015, pp. 110–11.

74 Schönenberger 2015, p. 117.

75 Special time limits apply for cultural property as defined by art. 2, para. 1 of the Kulturgütertransfergesetzes (KGTG) [Cultural Property Transfer Act]. The right to reclaim cultural property is subject to a relative time limit of one year and an absolute limit of thirty years (art. 934, para.1 ZGB). The statute of limitations for the right of possession is thirty years (art. 728, para. 1).

76 Bandle 2018, pp. 106–07.

77 See ibid., p. 107. A reversal of the burden of proof was discussed for this reason during the deliberations on the Terezin Declaration, but ultimately it was not taken up in the final text; see Jolles 2015, p. 140. However, at least for cases where an artwork was confiscated by the Nazis, art. 4 of the Washington Principles does provide for a certain "easing" of the burden of proof; see Section IV.2 in this essay.

78 Preamble, Washington Principles 1998.

79 See Entscheid Basel 2018, p. 162. On acting contrary to good faith through failure to observe non-binding principles to which one has voluntarily committed, see particularly the Handreichung, Rudolph 2007, pp. 288–90.

80 On the relationship between law and morality, see Entscheid Basel 2018, p. 145; Brülhart et. al., 2021, p. 130.

81 Entscheid Basel 2018, p. 158.

82 There is a nearly incalculable amount of historical literature on provenance research, and the same is true for the analysis of the situation in the legal literature. In contrast, interdisciplinary work is rarer. There are, however, certain museum handbooks that take such an approach: Deutsches Zentrum Kulturgutverluste, *Leitfaden Provenienzforschung zur Identifizierung von Kulturgut, das während der nationalsozialistischen Herrschaft verfolgungsbedingt entzogen wurde*, 2019 (kulturgutverluste.de/Webs/DE/Recherche/Leitfaden/Index.html); Deutscher Museumsbund, *Leitfaden Provenienzforschung und Restitution - eine Empfehlung*, February 2014 (museumsbund.de/wp-content/uploads/2017/04/2014-leitfaden-provenienzforschung-fg-naturwissenschaftliche-museen.pdf); Niedersächsisches Ministerium für Wissenschaft und Kultur, *Leitfaden zum Erwerb von Museumsgut*, December 2013 (mwk.niedersachsen.de/live/search.php).

83 In legal theory, the concept of the "wandering gaze" is used to describe the legal process of subsuming the facts under a legal proposition; see Engisch 1963, p. 15; Pavčnik 2011, pp. 159–61; Kramer 2019, p. 41. It enables the "equation" of the circumstances of the case with the statement of the facts; see Pavčnik 2011, p. 159. In this regard, in a restitution claim it is crucial to ascertain which "characteristics of the statement of facts" are decisive—whether the property has been looted or the claimant compensated—in order to subsequently focus on these questions. In the Curt Glaser case, the board of trustees also established specific criteria that guided their clarifications and assessments; see Entscheid Basel 2018, pp. 152–60.

84 Entscheid Basel 2018, p. 152; EDI/BAK, *Leitfaden für Museen zur Durchführung von Provenienzrecherchen*, June 2016, p. 2.

85 This principle certainly applies for proceedings in which the negotiation maxim prevails, in particular in civil procedures; see art. 55, para. 1 Schweizerische Zivilprozessordnung (ZPO). According to art 150, para. 1 ZPO only disputed facts are subject to the burden of proof.

86 On the different application of the central concepts in (art) history and law, see Goschler 2015, p. 50.

87 Art. 4, Washington Principles 1998; see also Stuart E. Eizenstat, *Washington Conference on Holocaust-Era Assets Proceedings*, February 19, 1999, p. 417 (commartrecovery.org/docs/WashingtonConferenceproceedings.pdf).

88 Baumgartner et al. 2018, p. 262.

89 According to art. 3, para. 1 ZGB, the good faith of the buyer is presumed unless it was not possible to act in good faith with due diligence (para. 2); see Uhlmann 2020, pp. 142–43.

90 Uhlmann 2020, p. 142.

91 Baumgartner et al. 2018, pp. 264–66.

92 According to the Handreichung, the presumption of collective persecution for Jewish claimants applies from January 30, 1933; see Entscheid Basel 2018, p. 149. The French CIVS additionally always proceeds in its investigations on the assumption that the claimant is acting in good faith. In its own words, it thus "lightens the burden of proof on claimants." See CIVS 2019, p. 33. The scope of this presumption however, and whether it constitutes an actual shift in the burden of proof, is unclear.

93 On the London Declaration, see Fiedler 2000; on the Bundesgericht's jurisprudence on the question of good faith in the art trade during and after World War II, see Candrian 2018.

94 The Kunstmuseum Bern recently also had to deal with gaps in provenance in connection with the Gurlitt bequest. According to the agreement with the Federal Republic of Germany and the Free State of Bavaria, the Kunstmuseum Bern had the right to decide whether to keep works with an incomplete provenance or return them to the Federal Republic of Germany. In accordance with an internal "traffic light" system, the Kunstmuseum decided to keep works with provenance gaps between 1933 and 1945 for which there was no available evidence or suggestion of Nazi looting (yellow-green category), but to return works with provenance gaps between 1933 and 1945 for which there was no proof but still some indication of Nazi looting (yellow-red category); see Stiftung Kunstmuseum Bern, Übernahmeentscheid, *Erwägungen und Entscheidung der Stiftung Kunstmuseum Bern betreffend die Werke aus dem Legat Cornelius Gurlitt mit nicht vollständig geklärter Provenienz*, November 5, 2021 (kunstmuseumbern.de).

95 A similar direction is taken in Brülhart et al. 2021, pp. 130–32.

96 Entscheid Basel 2018, p. 154.

97 Ibid., pp. 151, 154.

BOOKLET

This booklet contains a selection of essays from the German catalog published on the occasion of the exhibition

THE COLLECTOR CURT GLASER
From Champion of Modernism to Refugee

DER SAMMLER CURT GLASER
Vom Verfechter der Moderne zum Verfolgten

Kunstmuseum Basel, Neubau
October 22, 2022 to February 12, 2023

Bibliographical references in the endnotes are given in German and refer to the bibliography in the German exhibition catalog. References to page numbers and catalog numbers within the essays also refer to the German catalog.

EXHIBITION

Curators
Anita Haldemann,
Head of the Kupferstichkabinett,
and
Judith Rauser,
assistant curator, Kupferstichkabinett

Curatorial intern, Kupferstichkabinett
Amanda Kopp

ACCOMPANYING EXHIBITION

GALOP CHARIVARIQUE
Caricatures by Daumier from the Collection of Curt and Elsa Glaser

Kunstmuseum Basel, Hauptbau, Graphic cabinets, October 22, 2022 to February 5, 2023

Curated by Fabienne Ruppen, assistant curator, Kupferstichkabinett

CATALOG

Editors
Anita Haldemann und Judith Rauser

Editing
Judith Rauser

Editorial assistance
Amanda Kopp

Project manager, publisher
Luzie Diekmann

Production manager, publisher
Kerstin Protz

Translations (German – English)
Anna Brailovsky

Translation (English – German)
Kurt Rehkopf

Copyediting and proofreading German
Michael Konze

Copyediting and proofreading English
Rebecca van Dyck

Design and Typesetting
Verena Gerlach

Printing and binding
Grafisches Centrum Cuno, Calbe

Publisher
Deutscher Kunstverlag GmbH Berlin München
Lützowstraße 33
10785 Berlin
www.deutscherkunstverlag.de

A company of Walter de Gruyter GmbH Berlin Boston
www.degruyter.com

The German National Library lists this publication in the German National Bibliography; detailed bibliographic information is available on the Internet at http://dnb.d-nb.de

ISBN 978-3-422-98879-8 (German-english edition)

Cover:
Edvard Munch, *Portrait of Elsa Glaser*, 1913, oil on canvas, 120.5 × 85 cm, Kunsthaus Zürich, Kat. 229 (detail)
Photo: Kunsthaus Zürich

Exhibition and catalog are supported by the governing council of the Canton of Basel-Stadt and by the Foundation for the Kunstmuseum Basel.

Kunstmuseum Basel
St. Alban-Graben 8–16
CH-4051 Basel
www.kunstmuseumbasel.ch

kunstmuseum basel